T0146503

OVERCOMING OBSTACLES

When One Door Closes,
Another One Opens

ANDRE DONEGAN

authorHOUSE®

AuthorHouse™
1663 Liberty Drive
Bloomington, IN 47403
www.authorhouse.com
Phone: 1 (800) 839-8640

Published by AuthorHouse 05/27/2016

ISBN: 978-1-5246-1067-8 (sc)
ISBN: 978-1-5246-1066-1 (e)

Inspiration: A thing or person that inspires, an inspiring or animating action of influence, divine influence directly and immediately exerted upon the mind or soul. Merriam Webster Dictionary.

All my life, people have always told me that I'm an inspiration to them. I'm flattered by the compliment, but there are people more deserving of that flattering remark. Truth be told, I'm just an African American, physically challenged man who is trying to live his life to the best of his ability.

When I think of inspirational people, I think of single parents who are raising their children by themselves or people who were once healthy but then found themselves with an illness or a disability. Or people who are physically or emotionally abused by their significant others. These are just a few examples that come to mind.

When I was growing up, one of my favorite movies was *Rocky* with Sylvester Stallone. Remember how his character would always look beaten and then find the strength and determination to win his bouts? Well I consider life's obstacles my opponent. Whatever it throws at me, I find the courage and willpower to beat it.

People always say, "God works in mysterious ways," or, "He takes something away and replaces it with something else." Another saying that applies to my life is "God is not going to give you anything you can not handle." We may not understand what our purpose on Earth is; we just have to make the best of it.

This is how I live my life. There were two diagnoses for my disability. The first diagnosis was phocomelia. This means I was born with arms down to a person's elbows and no legs. I just have hips.

Then the doctors diagnosed it as congenital quadro amputee. They don't really understand what caused it. There are plenty of speculations that my mother used Thalidomide to help relieve morning sickness.

A person might think I'd get depressed with my type of disability. I'm not saying living with my type of disability hasn't been hard. I get down on myself just like everybody else. I just take one day at a time. I rely on my personality and intelligence to get me through the day.

For the past few years, I've been carefully reading my adoption papers. It's kind of odd reading about myself. For instance, learning about my birth parents is interesting. My biological parents had two children. They had me, and then they had a daughter two years later. My parents were from Trinidad. They were getting a divorce. From what I have read, both of my parents had reservations about me. If this is true, then I'm disappointed in both of them. Oh well, their loss.

Throughout the years, the one question people have always asked me is "Do you have any animosity toward your biological parents?" Honestly, I can say no. How could I despise people I cannot remember? I have no recollection or images of what my biological father looks like. All I read in my adoption papers was that he wanted to be a dentist and worked part–time as a security guard.

I have a vague image of my biological mother. All I can recall is a tall, skinny African American lady. I don't even know the sound of her voice. The sad part is that if she or my biological sister walked past me in the street, I wouldn't recognize them.

The only good thing I read in the adoption papers was that my biological mother placed me at St. Mary's Hospital for Children, which was located in Bayside, Queens. She tried to visit and bring me home on weekends as often as she could. I try to be objective and think about how difficult it was for a divorced African American woman with two children, one with a severe disability and a daughter, to find suitable living accommodations in the seventies.

So for the next six and a half years, St. Mary's Hospital for Children became my home. There were a variety of disabled children living at the facility. I was close to two boys, Willie and Eddie. The staff was very friendly. The hospital gave us nutritional meals and taught us how to live with our disabilities efficiently. I remember having occupational and physical therapy.

I learned how to live with my prosthetics. I hated using them; they made me very frustrated. I was in them the majority of the day. I would have to slide my arms into cuffs and use my shoulders to operate the hooks. My so-called legs were nothing but a bucket that I would sit in. The hooks and legs were mostly for cosmetic reasons.

Even though they were tortuous for me, I dealt with the ordeal. I learned how to write and feed myself with my prosthetic arms. Whenever I ate, I used plates with high lips or bowls. I can use spoons and forks, but my preference is spoons; it is easier for me to scoop the food into my mouth. Looking back on that experience, it should have been the first indication that once I put my mind to something, I could accomplish anything.

In the seventies, St. Mary's Hospital for Children was overflowing with children. There were more children than beds. This was a problem for the administration. They had to figure out a solution.

They say when one door closes, another one opens. This must be true because this happened to me. Who would have thought that a volunteer would have altered my life forever? Barbara Donegan volunteered at the facility. I have known her since I was three years old. We formed a special bond right away.

I looked forward to seeing her every time she volunteered. I don't remember how many times a week she volunteered. Even at a young age, I realized how special she was. She always had a friendly disposition and a smile. She assisted each patient with their therapies as well as their daily activities.

We formed a special bond right away. She came from a large family. She introduced her family to the patients. One by one, I slowly started to meet some of her relatives, who would later become my relatives.

Barbara was the one who found out that the hospital was placing some of the patients in a mental hospital. That's what happened to patients whose family didn't want or couldn't take care of them. I was one of those patients.

Barbara discussed the situation with her family. They discussed it amongst themselves and realized something had to be done to stop me from going to a mental institution. They did the necessary research to become a foster family.

You see, in the seventies, it was taboo for a Caucasian family to adopt an African American child, especially a child with a severe disability. Social Services was worried that a black child wouldn't learn about or understand their ethnic background.

I can honestly say that theory is a myth. The Donegans were not going to back down from this ordeal. They didn't care about the disability or race; all they cared about was the fact that there was a child who needed a home.

My family is so important to me. I went from having hardly anything to a lifetime of opportunities. They opened a lot of doors for me. Together, the Donegans and I discovered a variety of life experiences. For example, we learned how society has a misconception about disabled people as well as interracial adoption. My family taught me not to let my disability get in the way of whatever I want to accomplish.

I learned at a very young age what the true meaning of family is. Even though family members have heated discussions and sometimes-physical altercations doesn't mean they don't love each other.

You see, at first this was a scary encounter because I went from living in a hospital to having a large family. I also learned that it was okay for us to pick on or beat the hell out of each other, but it was another thing to let outside forces harm or threaten us. When that incident occurs, we rally around each other. Trust me, there are too many of us to take on. My relationship with my family is a good one.

When I moved into my new home, I had everything a child could ask for. I had a family who not only supported and loved me but gave me things I could only ever dream of. For the first time in my life, I had choices. For example, when my family took me to a store, I didn't know that there were a variety of cereals to choose from.

I also had toys and pets. I got my love for dogs from them. My favorite dog to this day was a German shepherd named Tuffy. They were worried that the animal wouldn't adapt to me because at the time he hated black people. It's ironic because we formed a tight bond very quickly. He became very protective of me.

When you're younger, you never truly grasp the concept of how much a parent does for a child. My biological mother may have given me life, but Pat Donegan showed me what life has to offer. She has played an integral role in my life ever since I met her. Here was a divorced woman who already practically raised eight children on her own, wanting to adopt me.

She said she fell in love with me right away with the things I could do. She also told me I started calling her mom after just a few visits. She fought very hard for me because she saw things in me that only a few people did. She treated me just like one of her own children.

She was very supportive of me right from the start. She was able to balance her job as a bus driver as well as be there for me for anything I needed help with. For instance, any time I had to go for therapy, she would accompany me.

I never once heard her complain about how much time she had to take off. I, on the other hand, hated going from Queens to Manhattan for all of my appointments. Those appointments pretty much lasted all day, whether it was for therapy or getting fitted for my prosthetics.

She tried to give me the best that she could. She provided food, toys, and an education for me. She gave me the encouragement to succeed. She never had any doubts about my abilities. If she did, I never saw it. She let me be me.

There are advantages and disadvantages of being the youngest of a large family. One advantage is there is always someone to talk to and get advice from. This can be a blessing or a hindrance because sometimes you really don't want to listen to what they have to say.

The disadvantage is you have to learn how to compromise and share with your siblings. Sometimes your older siblings don't take you seriously. For example, if you are enjoying a TV show and one of them doesn't want to watch it, they will change the channel. This only happened when my brothers would want to watch something more age appropriate for them. I didn't mind because I got to hear and watch some TV shows I normally would not have had the chance to see.

I formed special bonds with some of my brothers and sisters. I have a unique bond with Patty, Barbara, Brian, Dennis, Timothy, and John. I am not close to my sisters Carol and Joanne because they were out of the house when I came, and they were living on their own. Whenever they came around, they always asked about me and still considered me as their brother. They treated me just like everyone else did.

My sister Patty is the oldest. She is intelligent, nice, and funny. She has a huge heart and would do anything for her friends and family. Even though there's a sixteen-year age difference, we get along amazingly well. She wasn't just my big sister; she was also a cool friend. While growing up, she was very influential in my life.

Some of the fondest memories I have from growing up were spending time with her. Not only was she my sister, but also she acted like a mentor to me. I didn't mind because I was a shy kid, eager to learn everything I could.

I experienced a lot with Patty. When she says that she is going to do something, she means it. I mean, how many people would work a forty-hour week, stop and pick up their brother, and walk home to her apartment or house? Weather conditions never deterred her from her commitment to me.

I spent most of my weekends with her. On the way home, she would tell me about her day and what her job entailed. Her house was like a second home to me. I was very comfortable there. I would have to climb the stairs, and she carried my wheelchair into the house.

The weekends were always fun and busy. On Fridays, we ordered Chinese food. We would do a variety of things to occupy our time over the weekend. There was cooking, shopping, arts and crafts, fixing things, and so on. I loved it all.

My love for cooking is because of my sister. She always made it fun. Every time she cooked something, she had me assist her. Most of the time, the meals were edible. We always tried to cook something different. I was always her guinea pig. Lucky for me, I loved most of it.

Another aspect of cooking I loved was baking. Patty was the baker of the family. She would bake a lot of bread, cookies, and pies for people she knew. Baking was always an exhilarating event. We would take turns mixing and reading the directions. I would hold the bowl while she mixed. The first time we tried a new recipe, we would follow the directions. After that, we would improvise to make it taste better and more to our liking.

She used to tell me improvising is the most important ingredient when cooking. It's what makes a meal unique. This must be true because I always loved when we strayed from the original directions.

Not only was I her little assistant in her kitchen, I also helped her repair things in her house. This made me proud and confident because at first I didn't believe I could do it. I thought my disability would be a hindrance. Her philosophy was "What do you have to lose? Just try."

So I tried, and I loved it. We formed a great working relationship. We would put on loud music and get to work. She taught me how to put tiles on the walls and floors. I also learned a little plumbing. Whenever she didn't know how to do something, we would tackle the task together. If I didn't know how to do it, I would read the directions.

The one thing till this day that I'm proud of is stenciling the walls in her house. I would put the material between my arms and do it.

Even at a young age, I was open to trying new things. I didn't think it was a woman's job to do arts and crafts. I remember Patty teaching my cousins Eileen and Lisa and me how to make ornaments. We were so proud of ourselves. Again, I didn't think I would be able to do it because of my disability but was so proud when I was able to do it.

Socializing with Patty has broadened my horizon in music. I have to admit I have eclectic taste in music. Since there is a big age difference, I was exposed to fifties, sixties, seventies, and eighties music. I learned to like artists like Frank Sinatra, Elvis, Nat King Cole, Barry Manilow, Beach Boys, the Moody Blues, the Jackson 5, Chicago, and more.

We even listened to country music. I realize people might turn up their noses at country music but not me. Anytime I listened to it, I loved the beat and the lyrics. A lot of times, you can form a picture in your mind with that genre. Artists like Travis Tritt, Sawyer Brown, Alabama, Reba McEntire, and others really knew how to sing.

Every Sunday, we listened to the Top 40 countdown. We were able to compromise. She didn't mind listening to musicians like Huey Lewis and the News, Michael Jackson, Madonna, Debbie Gibson, and others. We would blast the music while we worked. It was fun. The only music we weren't thrilled about was metal.

My taste in TV shows expanded because of my sister. I remember every Friday and Saturday, we would watch British comedy shows. The British have a different type of humor than people in the United States. Whatever I was able to comprehend, I liked. I liked *Keeping up with Appearances*. It reminded me of *I Love Lucy* because of the things the female protagonist got herself into.

We didn't always watch British shows; we would also watch dramas. I was drawn to shows that had a mystery to solve. I loved shows like *Quincy* or *Diagnosis Murder*. I used to also watch *East Enders*. It was a British soap opera. The plots kept me interested.

Patty definitely knew how to compromise. She let me watch age-appropriate shows. She would let me watch all the comedy shows on ABC that aired on Friday nights. I used to love shows like *Webster* and *Just the Ten of Us*. I looked forward to them.

I remember after we would work for a while, we would take a break. Patty would make lunch, and we would sit down and watch the Sunday afternoon movies that the regular broadcasting channels showed. Some people might think I got bored by some of the movies they displayed. Tell you the truth, I didn't mind because I had an open mind.

I consider most of these movies classics. Movies like *Father Goose* and *African Queen* and *Guess Who's Coming to Dinner* had amazing casts. The themes were very controversial back then but can be used in today's society.

Another benefit of interacting with my sister was my love for reading. If I didn't like the show or movie that she was watching, she would make me read a book or a magazine. I didn't blame her because my two favorite words were "I'm bored." Who wouldn't do that in her position?

There were a lot of advantages to reading a lot. My vocabulary and reading comprehension were above average for a kid my age. The more I read, the quicker I was able to finish. I remember when I started a book with a lot of pages; I would groan and thought it would take me forever to finish.

The more books you read, you realize what you like and dislike. Patty likes to read anything and everything, especially romance novels. The day she put my first romance novel in front of me, I was shocked. There were so many things running through my head. I thought that only ladies read romance novels. But then she made it sound so intriguing and mysterious. My curiosity got the better of me, and I stopped thinking it was just for females. As long as there was a mystery with a touch of romance, I was in.

Sometimes reading a novel can be a pain, especially if you do not understand what a word means. Sometimes my sister would be gracious enough to tell me the definition of a word I didn't understand. Then there were times when she would make me look it up myself. I didn't want to do it because I was just being lazy. Then I realized it taught me how to use a dictionary. It also helped me memorize the spelling of each word.

If we were not cooking or repairing her house, we would go out. Patty would take me to various restaurants as well as diners. Even though I loved her cooking, it was nice to go out too. If something looked really interesting or good, I would ask if I could try it. It never bothered her since she already had four brothers before me.

After we ate, we went shopping. I understand that this is a foreign and torturous concept for men. Guys would rather get a root canal than go shopping with the opposite sex. I learned at a young age that it is not that disastrous as long as you have fun.

I observed what women like and don't like. It also gave me the sense of what I like to see on a lady. I was also fascinated by how sometimes ladies can just observe an outfit and realize if it fits well or not. It's also great when a woman realizes what she wants from a store, purchases an item, and leaves.

Patty and I also spent time with her friends. At first, her friends were uncertain of me since they had never been exposed to anyone with a disability, especially to the degree of my disability. It didn't bother me because once they got to know me, they liked my personality.

Patty made friends easily. She never saw their color or age. They ranged from a stay-at-home mom to a woman with a lot of tattoos. Trust me, every last one had a colorful personality. When you got them all in one room, you just sat back and absorbed everything. Here, I was educated in what men did wrong.

Patty was a lot of things to me when I was younger: a friend, a sibling, and a mentor. The greatest part she played was as a protector. There were plenty of times she sacrificed her safety for mine. When she had to bring me up and down the stairs by herself, sometimes she would slip, and we would fall. The funny thing was she always managed to make sure I was safe. Lucky for her she only got a couple of bruises.

Another memory I recall was when Patty, Barbara, and Charlie took me to Jones Beach. My sisters brought me into the ocean. Patty was holding me. Suddenly a big wave engulfed us. Patty was able to keep me afloat while she was under. Luckily for us, Barbara and two lifeguards came over to rescue us.

I attended my first concert with Patty and Charlie. It was a country concert. Poor Charlie, he was subjected to this music but didn't listen to this genre. Anytime we saw a concert at Jones Beach, my sister was the one who sat next to me in the handicapped section near the stage. He had to sit in the bleachers.

The first wedding I attended and participated in was Patty's wedding. I was seven. I wore a tuxedo with my prosthetics. Probably the only time I didn't mind wearing them. I was in all the family pictures.

No matter what adventure my sister and I did, we always had fun. Honestly, I'm not sure if it was just her personality or if it was for my amusement. Whatever the reason, I look back on these times with a smile on my face. What else could a brother ask for in a big sister?

I found out that Barbara was not only a great volunteer at St. Mary's Hospital for Children, but she was also an amazing big sister. The way she acted at the hospital is the way she acted in her personal life.

She is the youngest daughter and fourth child of my mother's children. She is caring, honest, and intelligent. She is the peacemaker of the family. She is a great listener and doesn't judge anyone without a valid reason.

I am so lucky that she saw the potential in me and convinced her family to take a chance on me. She knew the obstacles that I would have to face. She took me under her wing once I got out of the hospital. She made sure that I kept up with my therapies. For example, she would stand me up in my prosthetic limbs and help me get adjusted with balance. I was petrified because I thought I was going to fall. She would leave me there for a few minutes.

Barbara made sure I had a good childhood and foundation in life. The most important lesson I got in life was to never take money from strangers. Her philosophy was and still is that people are giving it to me for only one reason—because they feel sorry for me. She wanted me to understand that I was just like anyone else; I just did things differently. Occasionally I would slip, and I would get a playful slap on the back of my head from her.

Another of life's lesson that she drilled into my head was don't pay attention to people who stare at me. They just weren't used to seeing someone with my disability. Sometimes it was easier said than done. I mean I understand children asking questions and staring, but adults should never stare at me for a long time. Whenever someone gawked at me for a long time, she would stare at them until they looked away.

I'm not going to lie; I was your typical annoying sibling. One time Barbara paid for my drum lessons. I wanted to play the drums like I saw the musicians doing on TV. The music teacher insisted I had to use my prosthetic arms to play. He said I needed them so I could use the drumsticks. I despised those things. Eventually, we settled on a compromise. The teacher started me off on bongos so that way I didn't have to wear them. I lasted with the music lessons for two sessions and then quit. I thought my sister was going to kill me.

Barbara would accompany me to my doctor's appointments. Whenever my mother couldn't do it, she would stand in. We would take a handicapped transportation to them. It would be a long day. When we would get closer to the house, I would describe the house as the ugly one on the right. My sister was annoyed that I would describe it that way. She would reprimand me by stating that I was fortunate to have a home. Lucky for me, I only said it one time. I think most children doesn't like where they live when they are younger.

No matter how difficult or bratty I became, she voiced her opinion and was very supportive. The first time I was on a plane was with Barbara and my cousin David. They took me to Florida. I had a good time.

When Barbara moved out and got her own apartment, she still made time for me. I would sleep over there, and we would have a good time.

My relationships with my brothers were entirely different from those with my sisters. I got a male perspective from them. I looked up to my brothers in different ways. My brothers were like Renaissance men. They weren't your typical guys. They could be very independent. They could sew, repair things, shop, and cook.

Take my brother Brian for instance; he can do it all. He is an intelligent, honest, and responsible guy. He is my mother's fifth child and oldest son. Even though his sisters are older than him, he still wanted to be there for them. He tried to be a good role model for his brothers.

He was able to balance school, work, and family. He is a great listener and doesn't judge. He learned how to treat women from his mother and sisters. Besides his sisters and mother, women knew they were always safe when he was around. They knew they could trust him with anything and everything.

Brian is the definition of what every guy should be. I wanted to emulate him. I idolized him so much that I wanted to change my first name from Andre to Brian when I got adopted. My family convinced me that Andre was a good name and I needed my own identity.

So what does a little brother do instead? I asked him if I could go everywhere with him. I loved hanging out with his girlfriend, Ann, now my sister-in-law. They took me Easter egg hunting, to movies, and shopping. When he went into the navy, I didn't like it so much.

My brother Dennis is my mother's sixth biological child and the second oldest son. He is very different from Brian. He is a laid back, smart, honest, funny, stubborn man. It takes a very long time for him to get mad. He had to step in when Brian left. He would help somebody out if they needed it.

He is very persuasive and has a way of making people take his advice even when they don't want to. He makes people very comfortable when they are around him. He uses laughter and good listening skills. He explained my disability to children in a way they could understand. He used to tell kids that I fell asleep in line when it was time for me to get my limbs. Another line he used to say was that I forgot to show up when they handed out body parts. I didn't mind because it took the pressure off of me trying to explain.

My brother Timothy is my mother's seventh biological child and her second youngest. Once you get past the rough exterior, he would do anything for you. When I would finish my homework, he would play video games, talk, and listen to his rock music with me. I was fascinated by how he could build anything once he put his mind to it.

My brother John is my mother's eighth biological child and youngest. He loves working on cars and made a career out of it. It must not have been an easy adjustment for him, going from being the youngest to being a big brother. When I was younger, he always made sure I did my homework and went to bed on time. Trust me, he was very stern on these issues.

I was also fortunate enough to have aunts, uncles, grandparents, and cousins. My mother had four sisters and a brother. They didn't give me special treatment. I was closer to some of them than others. Some of my relatives lived out of state.

My aunt Geri and my uncle Percy were good people. I admired the way she lived her life after her bus accident. She was definitely a straight shooter. Sometimes, she could be blunt, and it usually rubbed people the wrong way. When I was younger, I wondered why she was so angry all the time. She was always nice to me though.

My uncle Percy, Geri's husband, was an African American man. He had a good sense of humor. When I was younger, he convinced me that for black people to keep their complexion, they had to drink coffee with no milk. For the longest time, I believed him. Boy, I was gullible. I wish we got to know each other better when he was alive.

My grandparents were good people. They lived next door. My grandfather was a very outspoken, ornery, and intelligent man. He didn't take crap from anybody. It was his way or the highway. Even at an old age, he stood up for what he believed in. For instance, I remember he would get furious with people who blocked his driveway; he would go out and confront them, and then one of my brothers or my uncle would have to defuse the situation before it escalated into something more.

My grandmother was a polite woman. She never hurt anyone. Everybody loved her. She was always there for her family and friends. She stuck by her husband through the good times and the bad. I loved talking to her.

My aunt Carol is my mother's oldest sister. She is a lot like my grandmother. She has a calming effect on everybody. She is a great listener. I have to admit I have never seen her get angry. She's the only one my aunts and uncle listen to.

My uncle Dick is my aunt Carol's husband. He is the nicest man. He is very laid back and serene. He is very intelligent. He's the only person I know that can remember the biographies of our presidents. I can recall him testing me on some of our presidents' famous quotes. It was very interesting.

My cousin Mary is my uncle Dick and aunt Carol's daughter. She is mentally challenged. I admire the courage she has. The saying that God takes something away but replaces it with another not only applies to me but to her too. She has a remarkable memory. She can recall things that happened years ago. Another good quality Mary has is if you tell her to remind you of something, she will not forget.

My cousin David is my uncle Dick and aunt Carol's son. He is a combination of his parents. He is intelligent, funny, and nice. It takes him a very long time to get angry. He will do anything for his family and friends. Whenever he tells a story, he can always make people laugh. He used to hang out at our house all the time.

I used to love talking to him and spending time with him. He was the one who got me into sports. We are huge fans of the Mets. I always loved going to Mets games with him. We would sit in the handicapped section. We would talk for a little while; then he would stretch his legs and walk around. I didn't mind sitting there since there were so many police officers around. I knew he wouldn't let anything happen to me.

I'm not really close to my other aunts and cousins. It's not because I don't like them; they lived out of state. Whenever we saw each other, we were very cordial to each other. They treated me kindly.

I have an extremely close relationship with my uncle Tommy and his daughters, Eileen and Lisa. Tommy is a special man in so many ways. He is smart, sarcastic, outspoken, and nice. His bark is worse than his bite. But don't underestimate his kindness; then he will come at you with full force. He is a man with integrity. He is there for his friends and family.

Tommy is another person in my life who helped me develop into the man I am today. I consider him more than just an uncle; he is also my friend and surrogate father. He treats me like a son. He took me on many trips with his two daughters. Sometimes I wondered if they ever got mad or resented me for sharing their time with him.

My uncle is the type of man that a father should be. Even though he is divorced from his wife, he is very supportive to his children. He tried to be strict but fair. He made sure they formed a unique bond.

The times we share together will always be memorable. Even at a young age, I tried to absorb the wisdom he put upon me. I look up to him. Our conversations are very diverse. Whenever he thought I wasn't paying attention to him, he used to playfully threaten me that if I kept being a pain in his ass, I wouldn't see another year. I used to laugh at that statement. Hell, I still laugh at it, and I'm forty-one years old.

Besides Brian, I learned a lot about women from my uncle. He taught me to try to look at every aspect about a woman. There are more than looks that a woman can offer in a relationship. I learned from a young age that it takes two to destroy a relationship. Another valuable lesson I can recall is you don't always have to sleep with women, sometimes it's just as good to be their friend.

Another time I can remember is the time he threatened to throw me in the snow with no shorts. We were down at his barn with some of his friends, and we were joking and being smart with each other. I dared him to throw me in. He tried to grab me, but I kept on squirming around in his arms. He couldn't get a good grasp on me and couldn't get the door open. There were so many good times I had with him.

Eileen and Lisa were more like sisters to me than cousins. We are around the same age. The closest cousin to us is Linda, but she lives out of state. Eileen is two years younger than me. Lisa is three years younger than her.

Eileen and I formed a strong bond right away. She is independent, honest, open-minded, intelligent, and kind. She and I were very mature for our age. We have a lot in common. We don't let many people see our vulnerability. We used to color, watch TV, and play video games. We would tell each other everything. If we needed to vent, we would listen and give each other advice. I still consider her one of my best friends.

I remember lots of times she would hate when my uncle Tommy and I would discuss females. We would admire how attractive they were. She thought it was disrespectful for us to discuss the opposite gender while she was in the vehicle or watching TV.

I don't have as tight a bond with Lisa as I do with her sister. Lisa has always been very helpful and cares about people. She never liked to cause any trouble with anybody. We always got along. As children, you never try to form a better connection with someone who is five years younger than you.

The great thing about having siblings older than you is you have in-laws. When I was younger, I was around my brother-in-law Charlie. He is a smart, athletic man. He has been in the family longer than I have. I always wondered if he ever gets frustrated with his in-laws since there are so many of us. I like talking to him because we talk about his job or sports. He likes the Yankees, and I like the Mets. The only team we agree on is the New York Giants.

My brother-in-law Jimmy is a smart and funny guy. I didn't see him much since I didn't associate with Joanne much. Every time we did see each other, he was nice to me.

When I was younger, Joanne, John's ex-wife, was a lot of fun to hang around. We would talk and laugh. For instance, I remember we went to go see *All Dogs Go to Heaven*. She wanted to see the movie, but she didn't want to go alone. I didn't want to go see a kid's movie, but somehow she convinced me to go.

Brian's wife, Ann, and I had a different kind of relationship. She is smart, outspoken, and honest. It was probably a huge adjustment for her to get used to dealing with my family.

When I was younger, I liked talking to her because she was easy to talk to. Even though she wasn't familiar with people with disabilities, she was very comfortable with me. Sometimes she didn't mind having me hang around with my brother and her.

As a child, I loved Christmas. Sometimes I would get up early and wake up everybody. With my brothers, it was very difficult to get them out of bed. Barbara made sure everybody in the house was up. My mom had a whole village that she built around the Christmas tree. We would open up presents around it. I had enough presents to open my own toy store.

It was a tradition in my family to go over to my grandparents' house for Christmas Eve. I remember it was definitely crowded. There were a lot of people in a small house. Everybody made the best of it. My family exchanged presents with those who couldn't make it to Patty's house.

The majority of the time, after leaving my grandparents' house, I would go home with Patty and Charlie. I loved waking up at her house on Christmas Day. Patty and I would bake in the morning. I loved it because she made sure that I had as many presents to open as he did. It made me feel special.

Holidays aren't the same to me anymore, but when I was younger, I loved them. Friends and family always gathered at Patty's house. People brought food and presents over. There was laughter and music. I would play with toys and share with my cousins Eileen and Lisa.

Halloween wasn't and still isn't one of my favorite holidays. On the other hand, my family loved it. They would decorate the house like a haunted mansion. They would display coffins in the front yard. My brothers and sisters would dress up. They even had me get in on the action. I remember that I would scare some kids because they thought that I was a mannequin until I opened my mouth.

Not only did I love holidays, but I also liked family trips. I remember going to the Catskill Mountains. My first time on a diving board was with my brother Dennis. He held me in his arms, and we jumped. It was fun. It scared the hell out of my mother. Another time I can recall scaring her is when I was able to hold my breath for three minutes under water.

Another great memory that comes to mind is when we went to Six Flags (formerly known as Great Adventures). There would be like ten to twenty people who would go. My siblings would invite one or two of their friends or a significant other. We would invite our neighbor. We would never have to wait in long lines since disabled people were able to cut the line.

There weren't that many rides that I was able to go on. I was able to go on the water rides two or three times in a row. It was great. In my youth, I didn't care that people were standing and watching my friends and family enjoying the ride as they were sweating and watching with envy.

One of the best aspect of being the youngest is you get to spend a lot of time by yourself. My brothers were your typical teenage boys doing their thing. My sisters were either married or dating or working.

During the week after school, my landlord or her granddaughter, Nancy, or my grandmother would let me in. They would take out my books so I could start on my homework. They would leave me something to drink and then leave.

Sometimes Nancy would keep me company. She is a smart, intelligent woman. There were times that I spent more time with her then I did with my brothers. When my mom worked nights, she would make sure that I ate. We would talk and have a good time. She was like an honorary sister.

If she couldn't watch me after school or at nighttime, I would lock up after her by using a hook that my family devised for me. Some people might feel that leaving a child with my disability was mean and irresponsible. I looked at it as a lesson of independence. I felt safe because I knew people were next door, and I had two dogs to protect me. Besides, I was alone maybe two or three hours maximum.

After my homework, this was the only time that I had the freedom to do what I wanted. I got to watch my television shows. I watched whatever cartoon was on at the time. I would also get addicted to the soap operas that were on. Surprisingly, the storylines held my attention.

I loved watching MTV, *Video Music Box*, *American Bandstand*, *Soul Train*, and *Dance Fever*. I was able to discover what type of music I liked. I will always be partial to old school R&B and rap. My all-time favorite group is New Edition.

Even as a child, I monopolized the telephone. It was cool because I had no one interrupting me. I felt grown-up and acted like a teenager. I would get in trouble though if I didn't answer the call waiting.

Now that I'm an adult, I look back at my childhood with fond memories. I also realize that it went by way too fast. People always say enjoy school while you are young. Or don't grow up too fast. I have to admit that I enjoyed my education. I have few regrets.

My elementary grade school experience was a lot of fun but nerve-racking. I went to P.S. 213. The first day was scary for me. Just like any endeavor I had to face, I gave it my all. My school had a combination of ambulatory as well as disabled students. They put the ambulatory students on the second floor and the handicapped ones on the ground floor. The only time we would interact with each other was in French class, during lunch, or in the auditorium for assembly.

As I entered the first grade, I thought I wouldn't know anyone there. To my surprise, Willie, the boy from St. Mary's, was in my class. It made the transition a little less intimidating. Being shy at first made me sit back and observe the students, aides, and my teachers. Something told me that I would enjoy going to school.

There was so much that I loved about my elementary school experience. I was in a classroom full of disabled students. The types of disabilities ranged from people who had cerebral palsy to emotional issues. I went from being a shy kid knowing only one kid to being one of the most popular kids in the school.

So much happened that I loved. One of the aides built a basketball hoop so we could play in the classroom. I remember that was the only time of the day that I was able to take off my prosthesis and play. Here we were, a bunch of disabled kids who crawled around on the floor and were able to shoot the ball into the hoop.

We would break into two evenly matched teams. A lot of times the games got physical. Some of the fights I saw were between disabled people. I remember this one kid who was very competitive and hated losing, so he would lash out at everybody. The problem was not only did he lose basketball games, but also he would lose most of his fights. A lot of classmates, myself included, really didn't want to associate with him because of his personality.

Since I had a laid-back personality, I got along with most of my classmates. Some friendships were stronger than others. I accepted the quiet ones as well as the cool ones. We went through a lot of different experiences together. I would sleep over at a lot of their houses. Their families would accept me for who I was. I made a lot of great friendships that would last most of my life. For example, I met my best friend, Juan, in the first grade. We hit it off immediately. He was like a brother to me. He was nice, funny, laid back, and smart. We would tell each other everything. I loved going to his house and having sleepovers. His family was very nice. I loved hanging out with them because I got to eat Spanish food.

Another great friend that I value was Jason Barnett. I met him in the fifth grade. We did everything together. Our families got along. We had a lot of things in common. For instance, we're both open-minded and have eclectic taste in music. We acted like brothers. We rode the bus together for four years.

Most of the time after school I would go over to his house. Jason and I would just sit around and talk about everything and anything. I learned about the Jewish religion from him. My first bar mitzvah was at Jason's. We used to talk on his CB. We would make up storylines and pretend to be the characters of our favorite television shows. He would always want to play the main characters, and I would play his sidekick. Our favorite show back in the eighties was *The Fall Guy*.

Then there was my classmate Robert. He was kind and would do anything for you. He was an incredible athlete. Like me, he came from a large family. He never cursed. We attended the same elementary school, junior high school, and high school.

Another great experience I had while in elementary school was running for vice president in the school's election. I was surprised that I won. It meant a lot to me because I was accepted by my peers. They saw past my disability and accepted me for who I was.

Another accomplishment that I am proud of is when I was runner-up in my school's spelling bee. There were so many emotions running through my mind. Luckily for me, Patty got me into reading. It helped me to have the confidence to try out. Too bad I don't remember the word that I missed to win.

In every guy's memory, they remember the first girl they kissed. With me, it happened when I was in the fourth grade. It was in the back of the auditorium during assembly. I had the biggest crush on a girl who was older than me. She was pretty and popular. Juan and I liked the same girl. The good thing was she liked both of us. She sat between us and kissed us.

Thinking back on that monumental moment, maybe it wasn't the most practical thing to do at that age. I mean, seriously, what did I know about kissing at the age of ten? All I cared about was this pretty girl who liked me. I didn't care that I had to share it with my best friend. I remembered it was nice.

Another milestone that happened in my life was when Channel 2 News interviewed my family and me. This happened because I lived in one of the oldest neighborhoods in Queens. Someone told the news crew how unique my family was.

Thinking back on that experience, I don't think I grasped the significance of being on television. All I knew was that Vic Miles, a reporter, was coming to meet my family and ask me questions. They followed my mother all day at her job. I had to introduce three of my brothers, three of my sisters, my cousin David, my brother-in-laws, Charlie and Jimmy. My sister Carol Sue and my brother Brian weren't there. They watched how I fed myself.

It was great having a reporter ask my opinion on things. I gave answers to him that only a ten-year-old child could give. For example, I remember saying that I hated when the news used to interrupt my favorite television shows.

I felt like a celebrity when Vic Miles and his news crew followed me to my school and to my handicapped sporting league. At school, they interviewed my principal and my friend Kevin. It was cool to hear great things about myself. You never really know the impact you have on someone until you hear them talking about you.

I love sports. I love it so much that my family found a handicapped sporting league called We Try Harder. There were so many different disabilities. The good thing about doing sports is I didn't have to do these activities without my prostheses. I was nervous at first, but I was willing to try something different. Unlike my drum lessons, I stuck it out for a long time. I did it for four years. It was fun because I did it with some of my friends.

In the wintertime, the league did bowling. We had to be there at a specific time every Saturday for about six months. My cousin Dave and sisters Barbara and Patty Ann mostly took me. Before every game, I would eat there, hang out with my friends, and play video games.

Once we began playing, I remember thinking about how was I going to bowl because I thought you needed fingers to do it. It surprised me when they brought a ramp out. I would adjust the ramp the way I wanted it. The founder of the league would give the bowlers some pointers. Someone, usually a family member, would put a bowling ball on the ramp, hold the bottom of it, and then I would push the ball. Sometimes I sucked, and the ball would go into the gutter. To my surprise, at other times I knocked most of the pins down. There were times they didn't cooperate. Those times, I would get frustrated, and whoever was with me had to remind me that it was just a game and not to take it so seriously. It was easier said than done because I have a competitive streak.

We Try Harder was like a normal league. We were split into teams. Sometimes you got stuck with people who weren't as good as you. When that situation arose, you had to remember to have good sportsmanship and encourage them. Then at the end of the season, we would get awards and trophies. There were a variety of categories. For example, you could get one for first place or most improved bowler. Another great category was the sportsmanship award.

During the summer season, We Try Harder did baseball. They divided the disabled kids into four teams. There were modified rules of course. For instance, when a ball was hit and it touched a wheelchair before the batter reached the base, then the runner was out. Otherwise the rules were the same. Some disabled children were better than others.

This was an amazing opportunity. But to be honest with you, there were some downfalls participating in baseball. I recall playing games in the heat and on weeknights. I didn't do well if the temperature was above eighty degrees. I hated to sweat. I hated having homework on school nights, especially in junior high school.

Baseball is one of my favorite sports. I realized that I was a better bowler than a baseball player. I used a plastic bat and held it between my arms. A lot of the times, I would hit the ball but just not as hard as I would have liked to. When the ball was hit, it mostly stayed in the infield. I also led the league in walks all four years that I participated. My cousin David used to tell me that a walk was just as good as a hit. The important thing was to have fun.

As a kid, you don't realize how much time and effort goes into making the league successful. You have to find sponsors, have fundraisers, and get family members to lend a helping hand. I know I didn't appreciate it; all I wanted and concentrated on was the prize. As an adult, I recognize how special it was to be involved in the league. It was definitely an integral part of my youth.

When I wasn't playing sports during the summer, I went to Camp Oakhurst, an away camp. Jason introduced me to it. I'd slept at someone else's house before, but it was only a few days here and there. This would be a great challenge to sleep somewhere that I wasn't familiar with.

It made the transition easier since I had Jason there with me. I can recall that my mom and Patty would drop me off in Manhattan. I would meet him at a bus; then the counselors would carry me up the stairs and put me in a seat. Jason and I would sit next to each other for the next two hours.

There were so many mixed emotions that were running through my mind as I descended the stairs of the bus. On the one hand, I was thinking, *Can I be brave enough for three weeks without my family protecting me, even though my best friend is with me?* Then another thing was; *what do we do at a sleep-away camp?* Jason told me the routine, but doing it was different from hearing about it.

A variety of children with disabilities attended Camp Oakhurst. Another thought that popped into my head was that it was huge. The staff was very welcoming, and it made me more at ease. We slept in cabins. At the time, I thought that it was interesting that some of the cabins were named after trees. There were five cabins on the premises, two for the girls and two for the boys. The last one was for the older teenagers where girls and boys were able to live under the same roof, girls on one side and boys on the other side. The staff divided up the campers according to their ages. During the summer, I slept in a cabin called Oaks.

Everybody was so cool. I tended to gravitate toward the popular kids. I formed tighter friendships with some better than others.

The last thing I ever expected was to have a girlfriend. She was very pretty. She was easy to talk to and was very cool. We did what any ten-year-olds would do; we mostly hugged and kissed now and then.

The counselors were great. They treated us with dignity and were not strict. The camp also had disabled counselors. I formed tight bonds with some of them.

The lunchroom was huge. You had to sit with your bunkmates during every meal. The food wasn't the greatest, but you learned to deal with it. It was camp and not a four-star restaurant.

There were plenty of activities to keep us occupied throughout the day. There were arts and crafts, music, drama, swimming, camping, and baseball. The campers were allowed to go on weekly trips to 7–11, and Scoops, a local ice-cream parlor. The staff scheduled trips to Asbury Park, the Monmouth Mall, and to Point Pleasant Beach, a local beach.

I loved most of the activities, except camping and arts and crafts. I always thought arts and crafts were boring. I hated camping. I hated sleeping on the ground in sleeping bags. I had to tolerate the bugs.

The best activities I loved were drama and music. At the end of a camp session, we were able to perform songs and skits in front of the entire camp. I thought that I was going to be nervous participating in front of everybody.

At the end of the session, they had a banquet. Everybody got dressed up and looked nice. I felt like I was at a fancy party. The campers were allowed to ask other campers to be their date at this event. I was glad that I had a date for the night. The younger kids had to go to bed earlier than the older kids.

It was difficult to leave at the end of my first three-week session. I tried to stay longer, but they didn't have the room. I never thought going to sleep-away camp would be so much fun. It was sad to say good-bye to my new friends. I kept in touch with them on the phone throughout the year, but it wasn't the same as seeing them every day.

The first three years, I went three weeks, and the last four years, I was able to go for the full six weeks. I was so happy because sometimes I would get bored at home during the summers. As the years went by, I started becoming one of the most popular campers. Just like any school setting, there were definitely cliques. There were popular couples and popular groups, and there was jealousy amongst us.

Teenagers were assigned to set up the dining room before each meal. We were to put silverware, plates, plastic cups, and a plate of butter cut into cubes on the tables. It taught us responsibility.

Another responsibility we had as campers was "bunk cleanup." We had to make our beds, sweep the floors of the cabins, and make sure the cubby of the bathroom was organized. This was a competition that each bunk participated in.

Each bunk had a counselor and a camper go around to inspect every bunk in every cabin. They would give points in every category. As for me, it was fun checking each one. I also remember that guys in my cabin were happy whenever we lost. Truth be told, we didn't try as hard as we should have.

As I look back at this experience, I realize one of the greatest moments in my youth was Camp Oakhurst. I experienced a lot of my hormones in camp. I can honestly say that I was definitely not faithful to a lot of my girlfriends or even to the ones I fooled around with. I was your typical teenage boy with raging hormones. Faithfulness was not part of my vocabulary.

Another aspect of my life was graduating from P.S. 213 and going onto I.S. 237. I look at my years at junior high as a learning curve. It was definitely a different world from elementary school. I can recall that the night before school, I had so many emotions running through my head. On the one hand, I'm always waiting for my next adventure. Then on the other hand, I worry that I will not succeed, and I fear the unknown. The best advice my brother Dennis ever gave me was to be myself and that entering junior high was another step toward adulthood.

When reminiscing about my junior high school experience, it is with mixed emotions. It was definitely an adjustment. I.S. 237 was much more crowded than my elementary school. You go from sitting in one classroom with a teacher teaching different subjects to having to go to seven different teachers throughout the day.

Another feature I had to adjust was being mainstreamed. This meant I was usually the only disabled adolescent in the classroom. This was very intimidating because I didn't know anyone there. The able-bodied students and I had to get used to each other. Another thing I had to adjust to would be getting a lot more homework, and the pace of the lessons was quicker.

One of the greatest parts of junior high school was that most of my friends from elementary school went there. I also made a lot of new friends too. I formed a tight bond with Eugene and Danny. These friendships would last for years.

Eugene lived his life to the fullest. He was charismatic, persuasive, funny, and very street-smart. We were different, but we had a lot of things in common.

Another unique bond that I formed was with a girl. Let's call her Patrice. Even at a young age, she knew what she wanted and how to get it. She was definitely a handful. She was very intelligent and very articulate. When she talked to people, she never made you feel inferior to her intelligence. She and I had interesting conversations on a variety of issues. She challenged me, and I liked that.

Another friendship that I will always cherish is the closeness with my friend Daphne. From day one, we hit off. We had a lot of things in common. Our favorite group is New Edition. I love our conversations. I used to borrow pens and gum from her every day, from junior high school to the day we graduated from high school. When I was an ornery teenager, she would say it was just I being me.

One of the most important decisions I made in my life was I decided to not wear my prostheses anymore. I asked my mother before I did it. I am glad that she understood my predicament and was very supportive. She also understood how I felt about them. She realized how much I could do without them.

There were so many emotions running through my mind the first day I showed up without my artificial limbs. On the one hand, I felt liberated and confident because I knew that I could do so much more without them. I knew my elementary classmates knew I had no legs. It was the rest of the school who were surprised.

Then on the other hand, I didn't know how my peers would perceive and accept my disability. I realized I was taking a huge leap of faith. I mean that was a lot to comprehend. They understood that I had no hands because they saw the artificial hooks. What they didn't know was I had no legs. It was definitely a huge shock to them.

There were a lot of awkward moments and gawking. I had a lot of questions I had to answer. Lucky for me, I was used to answering a lot of questions and staring when it came to my disability. Once everybody got used to the new adjustment, it was smooth sailing. I became one of the most popular kids in the school.

I was definitely your typical teenager. I was very ornery and started to not like school. When I was a freshman, I started hanging out with older kids. Two of my friends introduced me to the fun of cutting class. At first I was worried, but the more I did it, the more I didn't care. I proceeded to cut classes I didn't like, especially biology and its labs. Since I couldn't do the labs, I found science extremely boring and frustrating.

My friends started to be more important than my education. I can remember a bunch of us used to hang out in the bathroom for like two periods until teachers would kick us out and make us go to class.

At one point, I just went to school to hang out with my friends and stare at girls. I had huge crushes on so many of them. I started to realize what type of girls I liked. I knew I liked the ones who were pretty and didn't realize it. I tried asking girls out, but they politely turned me down. I believe part of the reason was in school, a teenager's reputation and popularity is very important.

Another factor I believe was because they didn't know how to deal with my disability. As an adult, I accept and can clearly understand it now. But as a teenager, it was very heart wrenching. My philosophy at the time was if I couldn't date them, then I would associate with them. In my head, it was better than nothing. The more I interacted with the girls I had a crush on, the more I realized some of them were better as friends.

Even though I would dodge going to class, I always made sure I did my homework and got the class notes. Or I would copy someone's homework. When I didn't understand the notes or homework, I would call one of my friends and have them explain it to me.

What used to surprise me the most was that I did very well on tests. Mostly I was a B to a C student. I would study extra hard not to fail. Maybe if I had attended classes more often, I would've done better. Science was the only subject I struggled with no matter how much I studied. For one reason or another, I couldn't grasp the subject.

Another turning point in my life happened in junior high school. I met my gym teacher, Bari, who had a major impact on me. She was the first teacher I knew who treated her students as friends. When she spoke, it didn't sound like she was lecturing or belittling you.

She introduced my friends and me to more wheelchair sports. She got us into wheelchair basketball, baseball, volleyball, and track and field. We practiced every day until we were able to compete with other schools.

It's one thing to play tough and be competitive amongst your friends; it's another thing to play against other disabled schools. There were games we won and several ones we lost. Lucky for us, we won more than we lost. It was also a good way to meet new friends.

Bari introduced us to the New York State Games for the Physically Challenged. My friends and I never knew such a thing existed. I was involved for three years. I'm always up for new challenges and new experiences. For me, it was a way to enjoy two of the greatest things as a teenager. One, we got to be out of school for a few days and sleep at Hofstra University's campus. Two, I love to participate in sports.

The N.Y.S. Games for the Physically Challenged will always hold a special place in my heart. There were so many disabled people of all ages. There were volunteers to help organize events. It was an amazing experience. There were disabled people participating in a variety of sports. I loved competing in the twenty-, forty-, hundred-, and two-hundred-meter dash, and wheelchair slalom. My favorite out of everything was the wheelchair slalom. You have to push your chair as fast as you can and go around cones.

One of the best things was on the second to the last day—there was a ceremony. I remember receiving gold, silver, and bronze medals for my disability category. I also received the New York State Games for the Physically Challenged Governor's Award on May 26, 1984. I never expected to receive such an honor.

As I got older, my brothers and sister Barbara started to move out and live their lives. In my opinion, it was bittersweet. On the one hand, having my brothers and sister around was cool because I always had someone to talk to. Then the positive aspect was that I didn't have to fight for the television. To a teenager, that's like winning the lottery.

Another great thing was if I got bored, I always had a place to hang out as long as my siblings weren't busy. I was happy that their places were accessible. I hung out with one of them for just the weekend.

For example, when Dennis and Laura Jean, his girlfriend and now his wife, moved to Pennsylvania, I would visit them. They had a nice, big property. It was quiet, too quiet for me. Out of all my brothers, he's the only one who makes me face my fears. For instance, he put me on his riding lawnmower. I thought he was crazy and wondered how I would be able to operate a lawnmower. My biggest fear was that I would fall and hurt myself.

He made me realize that there was no way I could hurt myself. He also made me understand that he wouldn't put me on the lawnmower if I couldn't manage it. Dennis told me I had nothing to fear because the worst thing that could happen was that I would fall on the grass, and the grass wasn't going to hurt me. He also taught me if I fell off, the machine would stop. He put it in low gear, and off I went. I put my arms in the steering wheel and was able to turn it. At first, I was petrified, and then once I got the hang of it, I loved it. I couldn't believe I was cutting the grass.

Brian got married to Ann and enrolled in the military. He was stationed in Japan. I was sad because I didn't know when I would see them again. When they came back to the States, I was a teenager and was too self-absorbed in my own life. Brian was stationed in Tennessee. They invited me to visit them.

I jumped at the opportunity to visit two of the people I thought highly of. I used to visit them during the summer for a week. At first, I was very nervous about flying by myself. I didn't know what to expect. Brian calmed my fears and reassured me that they would meet me at the gate.

I remembered thinking there were so many emotions running through my head. I was curious about how I was going to get on the plane. Up to that point, the only time I had flown was when I went to Florida with Barbara and David. He carried me on the plane.

I took the plunge and did it. I was worried how the airport staff would handle my disability. The airport staff followed my instructions on how to get on the aisle chair and bring me onto the plane. I was worried about how the other passengers would react to me.

It seemed to me that I had nothing to worry about. In my opinion, there's something exhilarating about flying. I felt relaxed and very independent. There were times when passengers would make small talk with me. Then there were times I just listened to music on my headphones.

I have to admit I loved Tennessee. I was so happy to see Brian and Ann. It felt like time stood still, and we picked up where we left off. They took me sightseeing. I met some of my brother's friends. They were so nice to me. I had so much fun that I didn't want to return to my life in New York. But in reality, I knew I had to go back. I visited them while they were there.

When my brothers and sisters started having children of their own, I was shocked and happy for them. I couldn't believe that I was going to be an uncle at such a young age. It was cool. I was very nervous about how my nieces and nephews were going to react to my disability. Obviously my siblings explained to their children in a way they would understand. Lucky for me, they accepted and loved me just the way I was.

I remember holding the majority of my nephews and nieces in my arms. I was very nervous holding a small infant in my arms. My brothers and sisters would stand near me in case their child was squirming too much. To this day, I am grateful that they trusted me.

In 1986, Jason one of my best friends, moved to Florida. I was sad he moved. At the time, I was wondering how I was going to keep in touch with him because I knew I was horrible at keeping in touch with people from another state. Back then, there was no Facebook or Twitter or Face Time. Not only was I losing a great friend, but I would be losing his family, who meant a lot to me too.

In 1986, Bari got my gym class to go to the New York Mets barbecue. My brother John took me. I couldn't believe that I got to meet my favorite baseball team and its players. They were very cordial to take the time to sign autographs and take pictures. I was also surprised to see how tall they were. It was extra great for me because not only did I meet them but they won the World Series that year.

In 1987, one of the greatest and fulfilling moments in my life was doing the New York City Marathon. Bari suggested that my friend Keith and I do it. We figured it was just another physically challenged race, but when she told us, we were taken aback and surprised. We never knew that disabled people could be in it. Then we sat back and asked her, "How many miles?" She told us it was 26.2 miles. We thought she was out of her mind. We had never pushed ourselves that far before.

She gave us the encouragement and convinced us to do it. I remember Keith and I looked at each other and thought, *we have nothing better to do*, and we were open-minded about trying something new. Thinking back on this monumental time in my life, it wasn't as difficult as it seems. Keith and I had to practice all year. During the week, Bari would have us push ourselves on the school tracks every day after school.

On Saturdays, she got us involved with the New York Road Runners Club, a club that helps train the physically challenged in order to prepare for the marathon. The club gave us volunteers to run with us. I think they try to match the volunteers with the athlete's personality.

First, we would start out a few miles at a time. At the end of a few practices, I started to get road burns, and they stung for a few days. Then they began to wrap up my arms in a cast to protect them. At first, pushing myself with it on felt weird, but then I got used to it. It also helped me gain momentum and speed.

Keith and I took the marathon seriously. We practiced hard every time we had a chance. We would give each other pep talks. We definitely got to form a stronger bond during these practices. We took one mile at a time and looked forward toward our goal.

The New York Marathon wasn't just any ordinary race; it would be the biggest race we had ever competed in. For fifteen- and sixteen-year-old boys, it would be one of the most exhilarating events in our lives.

I remember heading to Staten Island and staying in a hotel. We had to eat pasta the night before. We had to get up at four thirty in the morning to get to the starting line. The slower handicapped racers began the marathon three hours before the other racers. Keith and I were very nervous.

Before the race began, I had a lot of reservations about if I could even do this. I mean, a lot of people enter, but few people finish it. So I had to keep positive thoughts and think, *this is what all the hard work was for.* I had to tell myself I had competed in races before and to look at it like it was just another race.

The marathon consists of bridges, and you go through all five boroughs. So here I was in the beginning of November at six in the morning with just a sweatshirt and my arms bandaged up. So when the whistle blew to start, I was thinking, *here goes nothing.* In the first mile, you push yourself across the Verrazano Bridge.

There are several key elements in completing long-distance running: One, you have to know how to pace yourself. Two, you have to be determined and focused. Three, you can't panic and worry that your friend is ahead of you. Last but not least, you have to have fun.

That's exactly what I did. Bari ran with Keith. I ran with the best volunteer, Britta. She was with me during the practices. We had a lot in common, and she was easy to talk to. She became a good friend. She said that she requested to be my volunteer because we had an excellent connection. I felt honored, and it made doing the marathon so much easier.

People don't understand how difficult it is for the volunteers running with someone in a wheelchair. For example, Britta had to run with a backpack filled with supplies, such as more bandages and tape for my arms, supplies for chairs. While running, she also had to carry an extra wheel in case one of my wheels popped or got flat. Britta also had to keep up with me when I went downhill.

People asked me, "Was it difficult to do the marathon?" I honestly would admit that it wasn't because I prepared for it all year. The bridges were tiresome for me because it was uphill, but you get a little reprieve going downhill. The key to going downhill is you let the wheelchair flow. Ask any physically challenged person in a chair; the only job is occasionally you have to navigate it so that you don't hit anyone or any potholes or cracks in the street. Besides, sooner or later, the streets level out. Otherwise, it's smooth sailing.

While pushing your chair, many thoughts pop into your head. For example, I wondered if Keith finished the race because I only saw him periodically throughout the day. I knew he was ahead of me. That thought discouraged me a little. Britta kept on reminding me not to give up. It was nice when we caught up with him at the twenty–six-mile mark.

I never felt so relieved to see my friend and gym teacher. We saw the finish line in sight. We were almost there. Twenty-six miles wasn't the hardest part, it was the .2 we had to overcome. I remember going ahead of him a little. We did it in twelve hours. For those twelve hours, we will always admire and respect each other.

It was one of the most monumental moments of my life. Everybody was congratulating and hugging Keith and me. It made me feel proud. Once I finished it, there were three things that were pertinent in my brain: One, I was extremely tired. Two, I had to go to the bathroom. Three, I was hungry.

The next day, we had school, but I didn't go. Keith went and told me all about it. He admitted he felt like a celebrity. To me, the only thing I cared about was I was tired. My uncle Tommy used to think I was a fool for not going. He thought the girls would push me around and cater to me for just one day. I didn't need the recognition or the praise for what I did. I was always a shy kid.

As an adult looking back at the race, I still can't believe I partook in the New York City Marathon. I look at it with fond memories. Keith and I did it two more years. This time, we knew what to expect, and we were ready. Each year that we were in it, we got better and knocked an hour off from our previous year.

Upon graduating from junior high school, my guidance counselor proceeded to inform my mother that I would be better off in a high school full of students with disabilities. He also told her he didn't foresee me getting a job, and I would be better off selling pencils on a street corner. My mother took it as a personal insult for him to project his ignorance and prejudice toward me. She threatened to report him to the board of education if he couldn't locate a high school for me. Miraculously, he found one. I attended Francis Lewis High School.

I wasn't as nervous as I was entering I.S. 237. In my opinion, it was just another stage in my life. Most of my friends went to Francis Lewis. Like any new endeavor, you have to observe how things work. Once you learn the ropes, then you can master the task. I felt confident that I would like high school.

I made the most of my high school years. I was one of the most popular kids. I knew everybody from the faculty to the lunch people in the cafeteria. Unfortunately, I continued my bad habits of cutting class and copying my friends' homework.

While in high school, I was admitted to the resource room. The resource room was cool. I met a lot of cool kids there. In the room, the teachers helped us understand the subjects better. Some students, myself included, were allowed to take tests in there. This was beneficial for me because I needed extra time for tests.

I definitely would use the resource room to my advantage. I got along very well with one of the teachers. She was everybody's favorite. I would take exams and take longer than I should have. I believe my favorite teacher was definitely on to me, but she would let it slide, especially when I would take more than one period to take my tests.

Another highlight I used to my advantage was that the elevator used to break down all the time. Sometimes I would be stuck on the second floor, and I would have my friends carry my wheelchair and me down the stairs. Lucky for me, I had a lot of strong friends.

When I was not prepared for a test or didn't feel like going to class, I would use the excuse that the elevator broke down, even if I was on the first floor. I would hang out in the cafeteria for one or two periods, and then the lunch aides would kick some of my friends and me out. Then I would hang out in the resource room. If I decided to go to class late, I would beg my favorite resource teacher to write me a late pass or a note stating I was on the second floor.

Since I knew everybody in school, I was able to go to the special education trips, even though I wasn't in special education. I believe my resource teacher thought it would be therapeutic for me. She was one of the chaperones. In my opinion, I thought it would be just another few days for me not to go to classes. I had a lot of fun on those trips. I got to hang out with my friends and see how the teachers acted outside of school. In my freshman year, we went to Washington, DC. In my junior year, we went to Canada. In my senior year, we went to Orlando, Florida.

Francis Lewis had a lot of pretty girls. I had a lot of crushes, but nothing happened. The girls were still afraid of dating me. I would talk on the phone or hang out with them. Sometimes, it would bother me when I saw a girl I had a crush on kissing another guy. I would think *it should be me instead of him.*

One of my crushes happened to be the daughter of one of my bus matrons when Jason and I were in P.S. 213. When I found out who her mother was, I thought, *Wow, what a small world.* I thought this girl was everything to me.

I thought she was amazing. We would do a lot of things together. For instance, we would cut classes together and hang out. We would even hang out after school. Everybody in the school thought we were dating. We told them that we were great friends and nothing else.

I was definitely overprotective of her. Part of it was I knew her mother, and the other part was I liked her. There was more to her than met the eye. We would talk for hours. We hung out every day after school. I tried to be there for her.

I was so naive and infatuated with her; I even brought her concert tickets to her favorite band, New Kids on the Block. We were so happy to go see one of our favorite groups until her mother said no. Her mother didn't mind our friendship, but she thought going to a concert would lead to something more intimate. I was devastated.

My cousin Eileen hated her and realized she was using me. She definitely hated that she did this to me. She went to the concert with me, even though she didn't listen to them. We had fun. She was surprised how talented they were.

As children, Eileen and I were close, but as teenagers we were more friends than relatives. When she got her license, I thought it was great. Even though she had a vehicle and hung out with her friends, she always made time for me.

Whatever we did, we always had fun doing it. We would hang out once a month, either going to the movies or going to the beach. We went to Jones Beach during the summer. It was good exercise for me because I would push myself as we walked the boardwalk. The boardwalk was at least three miles.

I loved sleeping over my uncle's house because we would hang out with her friends in the park near her house. I knew some of her friends since they went to Francis Lewis. They would say, "I know you; you're the one who clipped me in the back of the legs with your wheelchair." I would say, "You didn't hear me say excuse me." The ones that didn't know me accepted me as well.

Besides hanging out with my cousin's friends, I also started hanging out with my own friends once they got their licenses. It was great when Robert got his license. He would pick up Eugene, Daphne, this girl Shanna, our friend Robert Thompson, and me. We were always able to squeeze six people in a four-passenger car.

We made Robert go everywhere in his car. He used to tell us that he wanted to be back at his house by midnight. We used to always convince him to do things even though he didn't want to. For example, we convinced him to go to one movie and sneak into another one. He was fuming since he always got home later than he expected to.

I can recall the first time I got drunk; it was in Robert's car. He was the designated driver since he didn't drink and he was responsible. It was a guys' night out. It was with Robert T. and Eugene. Robert T. and I were in the backseat. Robert was not happy at all, while the rest of us were having a ball. We would sing, Tony! Toni! Tone!'s song "The Blues" at the top of our lungs, blasting the radio.

We would drink in the Green Acres' parking lot. I can recall getting out of the car and wheeling around the parking lot. I didn't truly understand how drunk I was until I got into the backseat of Robert's vehicle. I tried to get onto the seat but with no luck.

I stayed on the floor the whole time. While Robert was driving, I kept on banging on the backseat. Eugene and Robert T. kept singing a variety of R&B songs. By the time we got to my house, Robert was fuming.

He wanted everybody to be home. I tried to oblige by trying to get into my wheelchair, but I kept on slipping. I ended up on the sidewalk. Robert wanted to leave me there, but Eugene convinced him to go knock on my door and get someone to assist them. Lucky for me, my brother Timothy was there.

My brother and my two friends tried to pick me up, but I would slip out of their grasp and quickly crawl up the street. While they were chasing after me, I would yell at the top of my lungs, "I am He-Man! I have the power!" After two or three tries, my brother was so frustrated that he lifted me up and put me on one of his shoulders and brought me into the house.

He put me on the steps and told me to get up to bed. Every time I would try to climb, I would fall asleep and fall down. He tried several times but had the same results. After a while, he just let me sleep on the floor until my mother came home.

My mother found it hysterical that she found me sleeping. She never imagined I would get drunk. She woke me up and told me to get upstairs and not to vomit on her floor or her steps. She said she would make me clean it up if I did. She didn't do it for my brothers when they were intoxicated, so she wasn't going to do it for me.

At that moment, those stairs appeared to be a lot as I managed to ascend them. My mother followed me just in case I fell down. It took me longer than usual because I kept nodding off.

I was never so happy to see my bed. As I stared at it, I remember asking her which one it was since my vision was impaired. She laughed and told me it was the middle one. I climbed into bed and slept like a baby.

When I woke up the next morning, I found out she had told everybody what I went through. My brother Dennis thought it was funny to whistle into the phone. I told him I didn't have a hangover, but he didn't believe me.

I guess that's what older brothers are there for, to tease you as well as give you great advice. As a teenager, I wondered how I was going to be intimate with a woman. I saw how ambulatory people did it, but how do people with disabilities have sex, especially someone with my type of disability?

Dennis told me that I was unique because not a lot of women are ever going to get the opportunity to have sex with a man with no arms and no legs. I mean, he even gave me my own pick-up line to use. He told me to say, "Have you ever made it with a black man with no arms and legs?"

I thought he was crazy. No woman would ever attempt to be that curious. He said, "If a lady is open-minded and can see past the disability, then she will." Part of me was very curious and hoped that he was right.

In my opinion, a teenager's rite of passage should be about attending the prom of your school. I'm glad I was able to participate. I was fortunate enough to go to two. One was my own, and the other was with one of my best friends.

As for my prom, I was very excited about it. This was an once-in-a-lifetime opportunity that I would remember for the rest of my life. I had to get the nerve to ask a girl to accompany me to my prom. When I was younger, I was shy to talk to a girl who I thought was hot. But I knew I wanted to go to it, and I didn't want to go alone, especially when my three best friends had dates.

So I took a deep breath and took the plunge ... sort of. I asked one of my best friends to ask one of her closest friends. We met her at Camp Oakhurst. She was extremely pretty and had a great personality. My friend and her kept in touch with each other throughout the year. I asked her to ask her for me to go with me. She relayed my message to her. She told my friend she would go with me, but I had to ask her myself. I took the risk, and she said yes.

While I waited for her response, I took the liberty of asking six other girls all in the same day ... just in case. To my surprise, all seven ladies said yes. Now I had to pick which one I wanted to go with. I didn't want to hurt anyone's feelings. I'm glad the other six weren't mad at me.

That night was good. Eugene, Robert T., and I shared a limousine with our dates. They were very shocked that I showed up with an extremely beautiful older woman.

There were definitely some positive and negative aspects of my senior prom. On the plus side, it was cool to hear that everybody was so impressed with my taste in women. I told them we were just friends. It was also cool to see my classmates in tuxedos and prom dresses.

When I went to the second prom, I went with a friend of mine from camp, and we formed a tight bond. We used to talk about a variety of issues. I was very close to her family. I was shocked when she asked me to go with her as friends. Honestly, I had a better time at her prom than mine.

Her prom was on a boat. I'd never been on one. Her friends made me feel welcomed and comfortable. It was rare that this happened to me because sometimes I can be very shy.

The nineties were an emotional era for me. There were some positives and negatives during these years. As I entered adulthood, I made a lot of bad choices and put my trust in the wrong people. I lost a lot of people who made an impact on my life, even to this day.

One of the hardest and emotional times in my life was when my best friend in the whole world died in June 1990. Juan moved to Florida in the middle of tenth grade. I was surprised and lost when he and his family moved. He got into a car accident.

When he died, I felt like I lost a brother. Juan and I experienced a lot together. Where could I find a male best friend that I could trust implicitly? We always had each other's back. I went to see my first rated R movie, *Krush Groove*, with him and his cousin. My only regret was that I never kept in contact with his family. To this day, I still get choked up because his life was taken away too soon.

When I graduated high school, I realized that this was a monumental moment in my life. Even I was amazed that I graduated on time. I guess even though I didn't take school seriously, I knew I had to stay focused and achieve my goal. School isn't meant for everybody. As I stood on that stage I thought, *this one is for you, Juan.*

When I was in my senior year of high school, I was introduced to a state vocational agency that helped the physically challenged fulfill their dreams and make them independent. I was very surprised by this revelation. I remember I had a counselor asking me pertinent questions about what I wanted to do with the rest of my life. For the longest time, I wanted to be an attorney or at least a paralegal. They were curious about why I chose that profession. I admitted that I believed in innocent until proven guilty. I also loved helping people.

After graduating from high school, sometimes it is difficult to stay in touch with your friends. Everyone now has to figure out which path to pursue. I found out it is easier said than done. Other people are fortunate to keep in touch with their friends. Unfortunately, I was not one of those people.

After high school, I went to La Guardia Community College, an undergraduate college. The state vocational agency helped with the finances, books, and transportation. They assisted me to achieve my dream in becoming an attorney.

College was definitely different from high school. There were definitely mixed emotions that I wasn't familiar with. I was always anticipating my next journey. I've always known at least one person whenever I started somewhere new. As I entered college, I realized that I didn't know anyone, and I had to make friends all over again.

College can be very intimidating. I'm glad that my family gave me the confidence to be independent. If they didn't, I don't think I could have gotten this far. I understood I had to take a different approach to my education. I had to take it more seriously.

In college, I had more responsibilities than ever before. There was no one making sure that I went to class and doing my homework. There were more term papers, and you had to try to articulate your thoughts better. If you failed to do this, you were the one to blame.

I buckled down and took the reins. I figured I had survived and overcome many obstacles in my past. Now I had to tackle this task like I did everything else in my life. It was time for me to man up and become an adult. I had to limit myself in watching sports and talking on the phone. I had to remind myself that this was the first step toward becoming a lawyer or a paralegal.

Luckily, I adapt to new surroundings. I liked attending La Guardia. I was able to make up my own schedule for my classes. I knew a lot of people. They had a good disabled department. They were able to give me a tutor and sometimes a note taker. I was able to have extra time for tests. The disabled department reminded me of the resource room in high school.

All my life, I had been an average student, never really applying myself. My grades were usually C+ to a B-. I knew I had to do better than that. I knew I couldn't get distracted anymore. Just when I started getting used to the curriculum, I was hit by devastating news that altered my life forever.

In 1991, I lost another best friend. Eugene died of sickle cell anemia. His death hit all of my friends hard we couldn't believe he was gone. For both Robert and me, it hit us like a ton of bricks. Eugene was like a leader to us. It is always a tragedy when someone close to you dies unexpectedly. To this day, I still think of him with fond memories.

After his death, Robert C. and Robert T., Shanna, Daphne, and I tried to do the same things we used to do. It wasn't the same without him. You never really realize how much a person has impacted your life until that person is gone. You just hope they appreciated your friendship.

Another bad thing happened to me while I was in college. The state vocational agency told me I had to choose a four-year college that would assist me in becoming an attorney; I couldn't attend a two-year undergraduate school.

While I was attending La Guardia Community College, Vic Miles and his news crew did an update on his series "Our Block." He interviewed me and wanted to know what I had been up to in the last ten years. He was very impressed that I had accomplished a lot at a very young age. I told him that life is what you make of it. To this day, I can't believe that I was on the news.

It took me a year and a half to get used to the routine at La Guardia Community College. I made a lot of friends, and I was getting good grades. Unfortunately, the decision was out of my control because the state vocational agency was paying for it. Honestly, even though I would have loved to get my associates degree at my current college, I had to follow their instructions. I figured that they knew what was best for me.

In 1992, my family suffered two major blows. My grandmother passed away. Then six months later, my uncle died. This was the first time that a relative of mine died. The world had lost two great people. I believe they are up in heaven watching over my family.

1990, 1991, and 1992 were emotional years for me. I was questioning why the people we love have to leave this earth. It's even harder to lose someone who never hurt anyone.

Even though the deaths in my life affected me tremendously, I knew I had to concentrate and do the best I could. I made a silent vow to myself to overcome any obstacles that came my way. My deceased relatives and my two best friends wouldn't want me to give up.

After leaving La Guardia Community College, I transferred to John Jay College for Criminal Justice. There were drawbacks in attending John Jay. On the plus side, I met a lot of great people, and I had my best academic year. I had three A's and a B with a 3.5 grade average. I was ecstatic.

I had a good relationship with my academic advisor. She told me to, "never use my disability to my advantage, to let people see the real me. Don't let anyone rule me. She thought that God gave me a special gift and I hadn't truly reached my potential."

There were definitely negative parts of attending John Jay. One was that it was located in the city. Two, I had no one to help me in the facility. I had to wake up early and couldn't go to the bathroom till I arrived back home. On average, I was out of my house at least twelve hours Monday through Friday. I definitely wanted to stay, so I continued my academic success. But unfortunately, it wasn't feasible; I had to think of my health. For this reason, I had to transfer to Edinboro University.

A friend of mine told me about the school. It sounded like a perfect environment for me. It was located in Pennsylvania. It was one of the highest adaptable schools for disabled people. This would be surreal for me because now I could have a great education as well as anytime I had to use the bathroom, there was someone to assist me.

I got to live on campus. This didn't bother me because I wasn't afraid to be away from my family for a few months at a time. In fact, I welcomed the new experience.

Edinboro University was definitely a different world for me. Able-bodied students and faculties were so welcoming and accommodating to people with disabilities. The school had twenty-four-hour care. It was mostly students who got paid and were also getting their education. The professors were very understanding of our disabilities. Disabled people didn't get any special treatment.

The only thing I had to remember was not to get caught up in the college trap. Statistically, students who live on campus have a tough time adjusting to the curriculum as well as balancing their personal lives. Whenever I used to hear this, I used to believe it was parents trying to deter their children from partying too much. But when I attended Edinboro, I had to admit that it was definitely tempting.

I made sure I wasn't going to be a statistic. Living in a dorm was something I had to get used to. My dorm had two floors. On the first floor was where they placed the guys with the disabilities. On the second floor was where able-bodied guys lived. At first, I kept to myself and made small talk with people. All I did was go to classes, study, and stay in my room. I tried to block out the music in my dorm room and people talking in the hallway. I didn't complain to my resident advisor. I had to deal with the ordeal. I had to find a way to block out the distractions.

I also knew I couldn't just stay in my room all the time and be a hermit. I had to find a way to balance a social life and concentrate on my studies. I found out it was easier said than done. Like any school environment, there are cliques. I just had to find the right one for me.

I tried to make friends with the people in my dorm. It was interesting because on one side of the dorm is where people were partying and didn't take studying too seriously. On the other side were the quiet guys who concentrated on their academics. It was like night and day. Unfortunately, my room was on the partying side.

I tried to make friends with the people on my side of the dorm. Some of them weren't always accepting. I did talk to some guys who were polite to me. I thought to myself, *this is disconcerting*. I had always been able to make friends with anybody.

So I gravitated to the other side of my dorm. This is where I felt comfortable. I met a great friend who made me feel like I had made the right decision to come to Edinboro. Let's call him Richie. He was a nice guy and knew a lot about computers.

We would hang out a lot. He was extremely easy to talk to. It was cool that even though we came from different backgrounds, we were able to form a tight bond. Even though he was smart, he never talked down to me. We always hung out after we studied.

I met another friend through Richie. Let's call him Lucas. He was definitely outspoken and a loner. He knew a lot about computers. Whenever I had a problem with my computer, he was able to solve it. Even though Richie and Lucas were friends first, they never made me feel like a third wheel.

People think that if you're studious, you don't know how to have fun. I could testify that is a lie. One time Lucas convinced us to go to a frat party. I had reservations because I had heard about how out of control those parties were and I didn't want to get sucked into the temptation. But as usual, I'm always ready to try new things. So I went to my first frat party.

The party was definitely crowded. People were drinking and dancing. At first, I was leery because I wasn't familiar with this kind of atmosphere. But after a while, people made me feel comfortable. I remember when some athletes brought all three of us down into the basement in our electric wheelchairs.

I had so much fun and got so drunk. When it was time to leave, I was curious about how we were going to get back to our dorm. Richie had to tell Lucas and me which direction to steer because we were both drunk off our asses. To this day, I am surprised we got back to our dorm safely. All I can say it was an adventure I thought I would never experience. The old adage of you never know what to expect until it happens is so true.

Just when I was getting used to life at Edinboro, I hit a major roadblock. I couldn't attend this school anymore because the state vocational agency pays very little funds when a disabled person goes to school out of state. My mother did the best she could, but then it became a financial hardship for her.

I was devastated and angry because Edinboro was the ideal place where I could have achieved a degree and then pursued a career with it. I didn't want to say good-bye to everyone. I was hoping for a miracle or any indication to help me stay. I wished there were warning signs; then I could have been prepared. But there weren't any, and I had to leave.

I came back to New York defeated. I was very angry, but I didn't let it show too much. I knew that my mother tried her best to keep me there, but without any financial assistance from the state vocational agency, she couldn't do it alone. At the time, they wanted me to continue my education in New York.

I just didn't want to deal with them anymore. I realized I was given false information from the time I graduated from high school. I was drained, and I didn't want to attend another school and start over. Every time I began another school, I would lose credits. I went to three colleges in four years. I had had enough.

So for the next year and a half, I just didn't do much. I hung out with friends, talked on the phone, and hung out with my family. My family tried to distract me. Sometimes it worked, and other times it didn't. At least I was able to read a lot. But it wasn't the same; I missed the school in Pennsylvania. But like anything else in life, I just had to make the best of it. Life was much easier when you were a kid. I was hoping for a sign to let me know what my next move was going to be.

I was very happy when my brother Timothy invited me to go live with him and his family in Florida. I figured since I wasn't doing anything, I jumped at the opportunity. I mean, what's not to like about Florida? The weather is always hot.

In Florida, I got to see how my brother transformed from a wild teenager to an adult. He had turned his life around. Timothy and I picked up right where we left off. He and his wife, Shannon, showed me all around Florida. I figured I could start anew.

My relationship with Shannon is cool, even to this day. She is easy to talk to and helpful. From the beginning, I was very impressed with how well she raised her daughters, Jennifer and Kelsey. They were cute and polite girls. My nieces took to me right away.

For the first few months that I was there, I just took my time to enjoy the atmosphere. I found it funny that sometimes people would put on a light jacket, while I was wearing a T-shirt and shorts. My brother used to tell me that the blood gets thinner while a person lives in Florida. I was wondering if that would happen to me.

I established a routine for myself. I would watch TV, read, and stay in contact with Patty and my mother. I would wait for everybody to come home and inquired about their day. It was okay at the beginning, but then after a while I was doing the same monotonous thing in Florida I had been doing in New York.

The old saying, life is what you make of it, is so true. If things were going to change, for the most part, I had to be the one to change them. I had to create my own life in Florida. Shannon did some research and gave me the information. At first, I was hitting roadblock after roadblock, but then I hit pay dirt and made an appointment with an agency to assist me so I could live my life independently, separate from my brother's.

Little did I realize that it was too little too late. Shannon was pregnant with my nephew Patrick. Timothy, Shannon, and I understood that it would be too hectic for me to stay. My brother worked a lot of hours. Shannon had her hands full with two young daughters and one on the way. It was for the best that I returned to New York.

There were some regrets that I had about leaving Florida. One, I would miss everybody. Two, I would miss the weather. Three, I wished I had not been a procrastinator and had been more productive in jumpstarting my life. But I will always be grateful to Timothy and Shannon for giving me a chance for six months.

Things were different when I went back to New York. My mother moved into a trailer in Amityville. My sister Barbara and her family lived down the road from us. My grandfather and my aunt Geri lived a few blocks from us. I had mixed feelings about living in a trailer.

I had to adjust to a place that I wasn't used to. It wasn't that accessible, but I managed. Lucky for me, I was used to crawling and lifting myself up everywhere. The positive thing was it was just my mother and myself. Sometimes it felt like I had my own bachelor pad because my mother had to work long hours and only had two days off.

We had a good system going. She would prepare the meals, and I was able to put it in the microwave. I didn't have to fight over the TV with anyone. Even when she was home, sometimes I would watch TV with her. When I didn't want to watch it with her, there was another TV in another room. I would talk for hours on the phone until she came home at one in the morning. I waited up for her most nights to make sure she arrived home safely.

When I did venture outside, I would wheel myself around the trailer park. I stopped by to visit my relatives. My nephew Michael and I used to play video games and listen to R&B music. My neighbors got to know me. They were very friendly.

I'm not going to lie; at first I had reservations about visiting my aunt Geri. I didn't know what to expect. Growing up, all I could ever recall was she would always be grouchy. I had a misconception of her.

Fortunately, I'm glad that I was able to form a unique bond with her. She turned out to be an amazing woman. There were more layers than I ever thought. She was very outspoken and harsh, but if you realized what she was saying, she spoke the truth. In reality, most people can't handle the truth. They would rather be in denial.

I don't think a lot of people took the time to really understand her. Don't get me wrong; sometimes she can be difficult. To my surprise, I found that she was easy to talk to and a great listener. I found myself looking forward to visiting her and my grandfather.

Geri and I not only hung out in her trailer, but we went places. We used to go to the movies. I saw movies with her that I thought I wouldn't like. For example, we went to see *Bridges of Madison County*. The saddest movie I saw with her was *Corrina, Corrina* with Whoopi Goldberg. In the movie, there was a character named Percy who reminded her of her late husband. Aunt Geri sat there and cried in the theater.

Until that moment, I never really thought about how difficult it is for a widow to pick up the pieces and start her life again. It was definitely difficult for Geri. I was glad I was there to be one of her support systems.

Not only did we go to movies, we also went to a couple of country concerts. I love going to concerts. I used to like going with her when she went to visit her aunt in Rhode Island. I thought that trip was going to be boring, but it turned out to be a relaxing trip. It was interesting that you could take your car on a ferry.

Anybody who truly understands me knows that I love long-distance driving. There's nothing like sitting in the passenger's seat and watching different sceneries pass you by, as long as there is someone you enjoy driving with. Geri and I had that in common. She loved taking me with her for a joyride. I believe she took me with her to get me out of the house. I look back on those experiences with fond memories.

Another fond memory that comes to mind happened in 1996. My friend Daphne gathered some of our junior high and high school friends for a mini reunion party. It was great seeing everyone again. It felt like time stood still. We picked up right where we left off.

Daphne interacted with various people, but I was surprised to see one particular party guest. Let's call her Veronica. I knew of her, but I had never taken the time to know her. I struck up a conversation, and we started flirting. We exchanged phone numbers. I told her that people don't usually call someone after they leave a party. We made a bet to see who was going to call first. The winner had to take the loser out to dinner.

I knew I wasn't going to call because I figured it was just a nice flirtation. All I thought of was what we were like in junior high and high school. We didn't socialize in the same circles. I was in the popular crowd, and she was in the shy and quiet crowd. Boy, did I have a misconception of her.

Three days later, she called me. I was very surprised she had taken the initiative. After she identified who she was, I inquired if the only reason she called was to get a free meal out of it. To my amazement, she laughed and didn't hang up. Thinking back on the situation, if I were her, I probably would have hung up on me.

I thought it would be an awkward conversation, but I found myself intrigued with her. We talked for two hours that night. I remember getting off the phone and thinking it could have been just a fluke.

Veronica called several times before I did. I found myself looking forward to her phone calls. I had to get past the image of her the way she was in high school and start thinking of her as a woman. I realized that I liked her as a lady rather than as a shy teenager. She told me that she was terrified of calling me at first. She was curious to see how I had transformed from an ornery teenager to a man.

Every time we talked, it felt like the first time. We opened up to each other and talked about a variety of different subjects. Even though, we came from different backgrounds, we still had a lot in common. We talked for six months and tried several times to meet.

One day, my mother offered to pick her up and drive us to the movies. I have to admit that I was nervous on our first date. I was hoping that the chemistry on the phone would be just as strong in person. Or would it be the dreaded friendship zone.

To my surprise, it wasn't. I'll never forget it. We went to see *Liar, Liar* with Jim Carrey. After the movies, my mom brought us back to the trailer. My mom and my aunt Geri went shopping so we could have our privacy. Lucky for me, my mom could shop for hours.

I couldn't believe that I was nervous. I really didn't know how to act because she had never had a boyfriend before. So I had to be cautious. We listened to music and talked. She brought me a gift. I felt stupid because I didn't know we were exchanging gifts. She brought Hershey's kisses and inside was a note stating "a kiss from me to you." I thought that was a clever way for me to kiss her.

But that was Veronica. She was an amazing woman. She had a disability, but that didn't stop her. She lived her life to the fullest with a smile. She also had a contagious laugh because when she laughed, you just wanted to laugh with her.

We learned a lot from each other. She taught me how to not take life so seriously. I learned a little Greek. She taught me to not settle for anything and not to give up.

Dating Veronica was one of the greatest moments in my life. She was like a seed ready to blossom into a rose. She was so eager to learn everything that I experienced. I found myself wanting to teach her my astute knowledge of the world. I also learned no matter what life throws at you, a person should attack it with a smile.

My mother and I moved from Amityville to New Hyde Park and went to live with my brother John and my cousin David. John thought it would be beneficial for us to live with them. John didn't like our mother driving late at night, and New Hyde Park was a lot closer than Amityville from Queens.

Living with John and David was a lot better than I thought it would be. It was like a bachelor pad. Mom mostly was out of the house five out of seven days. We would order out, or sometimes my cousin would cook. We watched whatever we wanted. John and David were always on the computer, and I would either be talking on the phone or reading.

When David moved out of the house, it definitely felt like I had the place to myself. John and my mother were always working. John was the perfect roommate because whenever Veronica came over, he let me have my privacy. He would come home, eat, and then go to his room.

At the time, I remember thinking everything was good. I had a cute girlfriend, food on the table, and a roof over my head. But I felt like something was missing. I wasn't stimulated enough. I kept doing the same routine day in, day out. Then one day, I was watching TV with my mother, and I was getting disgusted with how boring the show was that we were watching. She said to me, "Then do something about. If you can do better, then prove it."

I took it as a challenge not only for myself but for her too. I never knew how difficult writing could be. I was scared but determined. I recall thinking up a television concept, then thinking up characters. I would transcribe my story in my notebook and then put it on my brother's computer. It kept me occupied and focused throughout the day. Then a great opportunity came my way.

My brother Brian and his family came back to the United States from his second stint in Japan. They were in New York for a month until they had to relocate to North Carolina. Brian noticed that I wasn't doing much and offered to take me with him to look at potential houses. I jumped at the opportunity to go.

It was great driving to North Carolina. We bonded and talked about a variety of subjects. North Carolina was a beautiful state. We looked at several houses before he settled on one. In my opinion, it was the best one. The neighborhood had military people and their families. It was quiet. I was thinking that I could get used to living in a state like that.

I was curious to see if I could live with Brian and his family. I realized that I needed a change of scenery. He told me he had to discuss it with Ann first. To my surprise, she thought it was a good idea, and it was a great way to get acquainted with my nephews. But they wanted to get used to the state first. They promised after a year I could come live with them.

I'm not going to lie, I was very doubtful that they would keep their promise to me. People always promise one thing or another, but somehow things change. I went on with my life, but in the back of my mind, secretly I was hoping that moving was going to happen.

For the next year, I was on a mission. I kept in contact with Brian at least once a week. He would inform me how he and his family had adjusted to North Carolina. I was happy for them, but at the same time, I couldn't wait to move.

Even though I was so eager to move out of New York, there were certain people that I had yet to let in on my decision. For example, how was I going to tell my girlfriend that I wanted to leave New York? Here was this incredible lady that I was dating for a whole year. I didn't want it to end, but I knew I was being selfish and self-absorbed. But I knew this was something I had to do.

Telling her had to be one of the toughest decisions I ever made. She cried, but she understood. She didn't want to lose me. It was tearing me apart that I was doing this to her. We decided that we could have a long-distance relationship. I was very pessimistic about it because it is very difficult to do.

There are so many variables that go into a long-distance relationship. You have to have the utmost respect and trust for one another. There has to be constant communication as well as compromises between the couple. Part of me was wondering if I was capable of such a task. At the same time, I also acknowledged the love I felt for her.

Other people that it was hard to say good-bye to were my sister Patty and my cousin Eileen. They meant a lot to me since they were more than just my family; they were also my friends. Most of the time, it is very difficult to leave people you love. It was a tough decision, but I did it.

The year went by so fast. So in 1998, I embarked on a new chapter in my life. Brian drove up to get me. At the time, I was so elated that he and Ann kept their promise to me. I really didn't realize what I was getting myself into. But that old saying goes, nothing ventured, nothing gained.

To be honest, North Carolina didn't turn out the way I hoped it would. There were a lot of miscommunications, mistrusts, and not a lot of compromises. It was a part of my life when I could honestly say that I was fearful.

When I first arrived in North Carolina, I thought it was where I was meant to be. Here, I would get a fresh start. Living with Brian and Ann was an experience that I will never forget. I figured, what could honestly go wrong? I was with people whom I thought the world of.

When I lived in North Carolina, the old saying be careful of what you wish for was definitely a theme. I definitely learned a lot. The memories will always have an emotional feeling. I learned a lot about myself there.

When I first arrived at my brother's house, things were pretty good. It was like we picked up right where we left off. I had to share a room with my nephews, which I didn't mind. I was just grateful that my brother and his family made a place for me.

I also got into a routine. I continued writing my scripts. I would write during the day until my nephews came home. I didn't want to monopolize my brother's computer. I would have discussions with Ann after she came back from her morning coffee with her friends. When my brother came home from work, we would sit around and watch TV as a family. It felt surprisingly good because, at the time, I felt like I was missing that element in my life.

I made a promise to myself that I had to make a conscious effort to stay in contact with people who meant a lot to me in New York. Patty and I kept in contact with each other at least once or twice a week. It all depended on what was happening in our lives at the time.

Veronica and I continued our relationship, albeit long distance. It always felt so good to hear her voice. It also made me feel sad because I missed her beautiful smile. Whenever she came to visit me, we always had to stay at a hotel since my nephews were so young. I didn't mind; we needed the privacy.

I also tried to keep in touch with as many people as I could. It was easier to call people than to write them. I tried to keep in touch with my aunt Geri, Eileen, and Uncle Tommy as often as I could. Once in a while, I would call my friends. Whenever I was able to reach them, it was great hearing from them. I always wished that we were living in the same state.

I made a promise to myself that I wasn't going to waste any opportunities like I did when I lived in Florida. Truth be told, I tend to be a procrastinator. But if this was what I wanted, then I had to create a life for myself.

I got to know my nephews, Nicholas and Mathew. They were great kids. Even at a young age, you could see they had a bright future ahead of them. Nicholas had so much energy and was his own person. He excelled in sports and was tough. I was very proud to see his athleticism.

Mathew and I had a good relationship. He was so eager to show and tell me everything. He was very intelligent for his age. You could tell that he always was eager to learn new things. I was amazed by how much computer knowledge he had. Mathew knew more than I did.

Brian, Ann, and I started to prioritize my life. The first thing they wanted was for me to get a physical. They asked me, "When was the last time that you went to the doctor?" At that time, I hadn't been to the doctors in ten years. To be honest with you, my mother didn't keep up with that. So they made an appointment.

Everybody who knows me understands how much I hate hospitals. I don't mind visiting them; I just didn't want to go for myself. But they convinced me that it had to be done. So I relented and got a full physical.

When it came down to getting blood from me, they had to figure out a way to do it because my veins were not easy to find. They suggested that they get it out of my neck. At first, I was not thrilled to let the doctor stick a needle in my neck. Brian convinced me to let the physician do it. I gave him the authority. My brother distracted me while he did it. It was over before I knew it. It hurt more when they were putting pressure to stop the bleeding than it did going in. Lucky for me, I got a clean bill of health.

Then next on the agenda was figuring out what I wanted to do with my life. At that point, I wasn't sure which direction I wanted to go. I either wanted to give school another chance or get a job. Living with Brian and Ann taught me that I had to take the initiative. They paid off my student loans so I could have a clean slate. They wanted me to do all the research as well as make the phone calls.

I had no problem doing the research because that was the easy part. I get nervous and sometimes forget to ask the important questions. I was not used to it. Back in New York, my mother used to make the phone calls. So when I was in North Carolina, I wasn't sure if I could do it. But like the old saying goes, if you don't succeed, try and try again. I figured this was what independence was all about. I figured practice makes perfect.

I figured the only avenue for me to pursue was to get in contact with the vocational agency in North Carolina. They were the only agency that I knew who assisted disabled people to become independent. I had big reservations about using them again since I didn't have the best association with them in New York. I figured it was my best chance. I went to meet with them with an open mind and hoped for the best.

This time around with the agency, they made me feel very comfortable. I had a great counselor. I told her about my past experience with the agency in New York. She was shocked that I couldn't work out a reasonable compromise. Her advice was that this was my life and I knew what was best for me. We set up a realistic goal to pursue. I decided to go back to school and finish my education. They would provide transportation as well as a voucher for my textbooks. I had a good relationship with her.

Even though I wanted to be a writer, I understood it would have to take a backseat to my education. I wrote my scripts periodically. But I had to prioritize my life again. This time I realized that college was going to be more difficult than the last time. I had my doubts because I hadn't attended school for several years. I thought I was getting too old.

My uncle Dick once recited a quote from Franklin D. Roosevelt, "The only thing we have to fear is fear itself." When I was younger, this famous quote didn't really mean much to me, but as an adult, it has such a major impact on my life. I couldn't understand why I was scared. It's not like I had never gone to college before.

I attended Jacksonville Community College in Jacksonville, North Carolina. It was definitely a huge campus. Everybody was so cordial and accommodating to my needs. Luckily, a lot of my credits transferred from my other institutions. There were some courses I needed to take again. I spent plenty of hours at the college. I wanted to excel and get my associate's degree.

I knew this was a dream I was looking forward to making a reality. I thought nothing could go wrong. Unfortunately, things were spiraling out of control in my personal life. I never thought this would happen to me.

Sometimes living with family isn't always the best option. At the beginning, it was, but toward the end, it just got plain nasty. There were a lot of petty arguments and resentments that could have been avoided. I knew I needed a place of my own.

During this turmoil in my life, I got to know my driver. Let's call him Morris. He was the only bright spot in my life. He was the first successful entrepreneur I knew. He had three successful businesses. He shared a daycare center with his wife. He also had a locksmith business, and he drove me to school during the week. At the time, I was thinking, *it's sad that I'd rather hang out with someone who I barely know than be home with my family.*

I learned a lot from this man. I used to go hang out with him and go on some of his outings when he was a locksmith. I met his wife and daughters. His family welcomed me into their lives. I didn't feel stressed when I was with them.

He taught me two things that I will never forget. One, was you have to know when to act like a fool and when to not act like one. If you act foolish, then no one will ever take you seriously. I thought about what he said, and he was correct.

Another piece of advice he gave me was that I had two strikes against me in my life. One was because I was black, and the other was my disability. He said that society would always judge me first and make misconceptions about me. Morris felt that society is very cautious of African Americans. They will always stereotype us. If I was going to make it in this world, I had to learn how to act in the white world. African Americans had to prove themselves and overcome the stereotype.

He also informed me that society would think I was uneducated and helpless because of my disability. This fact was not any news to me. All my life, society had viewed me in a negative way. It was up to me to prove everybody wrong. I let Morris understand all of my accomplishments, and he was very impressed.

I never wanted to be stereotyped in a category because I realized that there was more to me than the color of my skin and what type of disability I have. I agreed to some of his philosophy. At the time, I wanted to grow and learn from what I had experienced and stay focused on what I needed to do with the rest of my life.

That's what I liked about Morris; he was determined, street-smart, persuasive, and focused. I was very impressed by how he was able to interact with people. For example, when he was with his friends, he would use slang words and have a good time. But when he had to put on his professional persona, he was very articulate and persuasive. He was a perfect role model and a great distraction for me.

After a while, Morris started to notice how unhappy I was. He suggested I move out and get away from them. I was extremely nervous about making such a drastic move. I didn't really know where to go. I only associated with a handful of people. Besides, there were rare instances that I was away from my family, and that was for a limited time. I had to make the right decision for me.

I knew before I embarked on this new journey I had to discuss this with my girlfriend. I had to approach this topic very cautiously; I didn't know what kind of reaction I would get. In the end, she was very supportive of my decision. She wanted the best for me. She wanted to make me happy.

I also asked my sister Patty's opinion on the situation. She realized how unhappy and frustrated I was. She also made me realize that I was an adult, and sometimes a person has to make difficult decisions.

The next step I had to do was discuss this option with Brian and Ann. To be honest, I was pretty nervous. On the one hand, I didn't want them to feel like I was ungrateful for everything they did for me. Part of me felt guilty for leaving.

I talked to them. We agreed that it was best for everyone involved. They just asked the basics of when and where I was going to live. In the back of my mind, I felt hurt and betrayed. They didn't try to talk me out of leaving. In the back of my mind, I should have realized that it was time to be on my own and be independent.

When I left Brian's house, there were a lot of mixed emotions running around inside my head. I had anger and disappointment toward them. I thought at least at the eleventh hour, they would stop me, and we could have worked out some kind of compromise. At the time, I thought family was supposed to be there for each other through the good and bad times. Secretly I hoped I didn't damage our relationship.

All my life, I always felt I could accomplish anything because I had the confidence and my family to support me. When I left, I realized I was entering unfamiliar territory. I didn't know what to expect. All I knew was that I had to rely on and trust strangers to assist me with everything. I was petrified. The only one who helped me out tremendously was Morris.

Morris found me a place. He knew of a guy who needed a roommate. I met my roommate. Let's call him Luther. I met him a few times while I hung out with Morris. He seemed like a nice man at the time. I was so ecstatic that I found someone who could share half of the bills with me. I was thinking this was a step in the right direction and toward becoming independent.

I loved my two-bedroom apartment. It already had Morris's furniture in it. He let me buy it off of him for two hundred and fifty dollars. I thought, *Where else could I have gotten a water bed, leather couch, TV, TV stand, and pots and pans for such a great bargain?* I was thinking that he came into my life for a reason, and I was thankful for him introducing me to Luther.

My relationship with Luther was definitely an interesting one. We were definitely the odd couple. He was in his late forties, an African American man who was set in his ways and raised in the projects. He had a quick temper. Then there was me who was in my late twenties, disabled, outspoken, reasonable, sometimes gullible, and raised in a white family.

I was so fortunate to have an apartment that I could share with someone. At first, the age difference and our lifestyle didn't come between us. We were able to coexist. I went to college during the day and still went out with Morris on one of his business trips. Luther would do whatever he did during the day. I would ask him sometimes how his day was, mostly out of courtesy. There were some good times that my roommate and I had.

I got to meet some of his relatives. His sister and nephews lived right next door. His sister was one of the nicest ladies I ever met. She was short but demanded respect. I loved talking with his nephews. One of his nephews was really cool and would cut my hair for free. He did a great job.

I didn't mind the age difference since I always hung out with people from different age groups. At the beginning, Luther would assist me with my hygiene and cooking. I have to admit he was a very good cook. I tried things I had never tried before. For instance, I tried grits and was surprised that I liked them a lot. He helped me until I was able to get with a home-health agency.

That was another thing I had to get used to. I had to rely on strangers seeing me naked. I remember being very paranoid of this situation. Sometimes in the media you hear about home-health aides taking advantage of their clients. I also wasn't sure what I was supposed to do with a personal care assistant for a couple of hours a day.

This was a big adjustment, but there was no other option for me. I had to get used to having different aides coming in and explaining what they had to do for me on a regular basis. I had to explain my disability to new aides every time they met with me. I didn't mind since I had to do it my entire life. After a while, I got used to it. Some of the aides were easier to talk to than others.

I had to learn that having a roommate who was much older than you could be stressful at times. I had to learn how to compromise really quickly. For instance, having a home-health aide coming into our apartment was a huge transition for him as well as for myself. He figured they would come in and cook for the both of us. I tried to explain that they were there to take care of me and not him.

Luther didn't understand the meaning of compromise and reason. Since he was much older than Morris, his nephews, and I, he never took our advice seriously. The only one he reasonably listened to was his sister. The rest of us, he would tell us to mind our business.

What I thought was going to be great started to turn into a nightmare. I felt embarrassed because I couldn't get a steady aide for months. I had to explain to the home-health agency about his attitude.

Initially, when you have a roommate, you expect them to share half the bills. I tried to talk to him rationally, but that was useless. He figured since he helped me whenever the aides weren't around, he didn't feel obligated. I tried to make him see that one thing had nothing to do with the other. He thought I was ungrateful.

It was getting very tiresome living with Luther. The age difference and our background started to show. I could recall that anytime we had an interesting conversation, our philosophies would clash. He had an old-school street-smart way of thinking, and I had an educational approach to things. Morris tried to play mediator a lot.

To this day, I don't understand what made me continue most of our disagreements. I should have realized that people have a right to their opinions. I may not have agreed with it, but that does not make them a bad person.

Throughout the ordeal, I'm glad that Veronica wasn't able to witness the strained relationship I had with my roommate. Every time she came to visit, we would stay at a hotel. Trust me, I would have preferred to entertain her in my own apartment than spend money on a hotel. But I couldn't risk his unpredictable personality on her. I knew she couldn't handle it.

At the same time, I wished I had a familiar face to tell me everything was going to be all right. Veronica did her best to ease my tension. It was difficult to do it long distance. Part of me was thinking and hoping for a solution throughout all of this.

During this chaotic time in my life, I was able to keep a steady home-health aide. Her name was Tina. She wasn't intimidated by my roommate's outtakes. She was polite and observed everything. She saw that I was in a bad situation. We became friends right away. She was so easy to talk to. I always looked forward to her shift.

She noticed that things were starting to become overwhelming for me. To relieve some of the tension, she would bring me to her house on Sundays, and I hung out with her family. I loved spending time with them. I was curious to see how she interacted in her personal life.

To my amazement, she was the same way. At the time, I thought it couldn't have been easy for her. She was juggling so many things. She held two jobs and was a mother and a wife. She made it look so easy. I was impressed.

At the time, I was probably more nervous about meeting her family than they were about meeting me. I was so happy that they made me feel comfortable when I met them. Her oldest son, Michael, was very outgoing and made me feel welcomed. He played video games with me. It took a little while for her youngest, Dakota and McKenzie, to warm up to me. They were shy and tried to understand the concept of someone with no limbs. Her husband, Ray, and I got along.

Being with Tina and her family made me forget all my troubles ... well at least for one day. They made me feel so comfortable that I never wanted to return to my apartment again. But unfortunately, I couldn't neglect my responsibilities as an adult. Even though I wanted to so badly.

I truly started to resent my life and the people in it. I recall the moment I had to do something to make myself happy. It was one of the toughest times in my life. Someone stole three hundred dollars from my bank account. I couldn't believe this was happening to me.

There were so many emotions running through me at the time. I felt betrayed that someone I knew would be so cruel. Everyone knew my financial situation. I was scared because I didn't know whom to trust. People whom I thought were my friends weren't really. I wanted to severely hurt somebody. I wanted to go somewhere and feel safe again.

The only safe haven I knew was to turn to my family. First, I tried my brother Brian to see if he would assist me. The only thing he did was drive me to the police department so I could report the crime.

When I went to the police department, they tried to be sympathetic, but they didn't have any solution for me. They did inform me whoever did steal the money was very calculating. The perpetrator went to an ATM machine that didn't have a camera. They couldn't do anything else for me unless I had a suspect.

Unfortunately there were too many suspects. Everyone that helped me had access to my debit card. Every time I needed to go to the bank or ATM machine, they convinced me that it was easier or quicker for them to go than putting me in their vehicle. At the time, it seemed like a reasonable explanation.

When the word spread that I was at the police station, people started acting differently toward me. They were accusing me of being racist because the majority of the people I was around were black. I tried to explain that it had nothing to do with the color of a person's skin; it had to do with someone misleading me.

After this horrible and stressful time, I thought Brian would ask me to return to his home. I assumed that he was worried about my safety. I wanted and needed to feel protected again. But at the same time, my pride got in the way of me coming out and asking him.

Then I turned to certain members of my family in New York. I thought they would never let me down. I was definitely wrong. They said it was a long ride, and they couldn't take the time off from work. I understood that people couldn't come during the week, but I was hoping someone would try to do a three-day weekend. I pleaded my case but to no avail. They truly didn't understand the dire situation I was really in.

Tina couldn't believe as big as my family was that there was no one who could take the time to help me. Against company policy, she wanted me to live with her family and her. I had to figure out what would be the best decision for me. All I knew was that I couldn't live with my roommate anymore. Tina was my only and best option I had at the time.

But I also knew I had responsibilities to certain people. The first person I had to discuss moving out with was Morris. I needed him to understand I was grateful for everything that I learned from him. I was thankful for the opportunity of having my first apartment. To my surprise, he was very understanding and wished me luck.

When the day came for me to move out, I had mixed emotions. It wasn't so much about me missing my roommate but the sense that I had something that was partially mine. I wanted my own privacy.

There were so many things I had to do the day I moved out. Tina and Ray moved all of my stuff out of the apartment and into storage. I took my name off of all the bills. I notified my sister Patty, my mother, and Veronica of my new living arrangements.

I couldn't believe how much pressure was taken off of me when I went to live with Tina and Ray. I thought they made me feel comfortable just because I was just visiting as a friend. I was so lucky that wasn't the case.

I also knew I didn't want to make the same mistake I had living with another family. I had to learn to compromise all over again. But fortunately for me, it was an easy adjustment. Tina and her family were very laid back when it came to rules.

I remember the first night living with Tina as if it was yesterday. We sat up and talked until two in the morning. There wasn't a topic that we didn't discuss. For instance, she was only going to charge me the same rate I was paying when I had my apartment. I thought that was admirable.

I had to share a room with Michael, which I didn't mind. All my life, I had to share sleeping arrangements with somebody. We shared a bunk bed. To my amazement, he never once complained about my snoring.

Tina had to confess to her employers after a week of my whereabouts. They knew we were close and figured that I was living with her. Fortunately for both of us, they were sympathetic to my situation. They compromised with us. They would send another aide out to her house to help me, but she couldn't be my aide because it was against company policy for an aide and client to live together. We thought it was a reasonable agreement.

I started to think of Tina's home as my own. During the day, I wrote my script, read a book, and talked to my girlfriend. Talking to her was the highlight of my day. Sometimes I would contact my sister Patty, but mostly I waited till the weekend.

I even enjoyed talking to my new aide; she was a nice little old woman. It was such a relief that I didn't have to worry about someone disrespecting me. The aide and I started to bond. I even showed her a couple of pages of my script. She found it fascinating that I did it without even going to school. She enjoyed it and thought I had potential. It made me feel good.

I was curious about how everybody's day was when everybody came home. They told me. At nighttime, I would either read or watch TV with everybody. I also loved the times that Tina and I would talk after everyone went to bed. I was very happy there until I found out that she and her family were returning to their home state, Maine.

At the time, *I was thinking every time I get used to a place, something drastically alternates my life*. I was worried that there were no options for me. For instance, I realized there were no options for me in North Carolina. I didn't have any relatives that I could talk to that could assist me. Then the other viable option was to return to New York. But then I figured, who would come and get me since no one did when my money was stolen?

The original plan was for Tina to drop me off at Patty's house on the way to Maine. I didn't want to go back to New York because I knew what it was like for someone with my type of disability. Besides, I hadn't had much success since I was a child.

I started inquiring about life in Maine. Tina filled me in on her life in the state. It sounded good, and it seemed like a perfect fit for me to start my life over again. At first, I didn't know how to ask if I could tag along. To this day, I strongly believe that she knew I wanted to come, but I had to be the one to say it. I took the plunge and asked her.

I was so happy she let me come with her. I informed my girlfriend, Patty, and my mother that I was headed to Maine. At first, everybody was shocked, considering that I didn't know what the lifestyle was going to be. I figured nothing ventured, nothing gained.

As I look back at my life in North Carolina, there were some positive and negative aspects. From 1998 to 2001, I learned some of life's hard lessons. I've had disappointments and setbacks but nothing like what occurred in that state.

Even though I was a man in my late twenties, I hadn't grown up. I always had my family to depend on and find solutions for me. When I moved out of New York, I thought that would continue. I had to learn to depend on others and try to trust my instinct.

Unfortunately, I made some huge and difficult decisions. I put my trust in the wrong people. I idolized too many people and was mad when they let me down. I also understood that I was naïve and gullible.

I was looking for solutions without asking the right questions. Or I didn't care about the consequences. All I needed and wanted was for an easy way out. But at the same time, there are no guarantees in life.

The lessons I learned from North Carolina have changed me for the better. I know how to act in certain situations. I should never let my emotions get the best of me. I can depend on people a little bit but not all the time.

Whenever I think about my time in Maine, it always puts a smile on my face. It was the best three and a half years of my life. It ranks right up there with being adopted, finishing all three of my marathons, and losing my virginity.

Maine was where I learned that family doesn't necessarily mean blood related. There are people who care about you that are not family. There was a reason Tina and her family entered my life. I needed to feel like I was part of something and trust people again.

In February 2001, I arrived in Maine. I can recall it like it was yesterday. We arrived in the middle of a snowstorm. It was freezing. It felt good to see snow again.

There were so many different emotions running through my head. The most important question was, was I being impulsive and not thinking things through? I also remember I thought I was going to feel uncomfortable and out of my element. I also was thinking, *who moves to another state just knowing five people?* Tina and her whole family made me so comfortable as soon as I arrived. Right from the beginning, I knew I had made the right decision.

It was nice meeting everyone. We stayed at Rose, Tina's mother's, house until we found a place for us to live. I liked her right away. She was very outspoken, and what you saw was what you got. She was tough but fair. She also had a good heart. When I first got there, she bought me a jacket. I was so surprised that she bought a complete stranger a gift the next day.

I liked Tina's father, Dickie. He was an outspoken, easygoing, and honest man. He was easy to talk to. He demanded respect and got it. He was always nice to me whenever he saw me.

Tina's sisters, Missy and Lynn, are great women. They are just like Tina and her mother. They were honest, outspoken, kind, and independent. Like their older sibling, they were able to balance their professional lives as well as their personal lives. They demanded respect from everyone they met. Whenever they saw me, they were friendly and probably thought of me like an honorary brother. At least I hope they did since I thought of them like honorary sisters.

The first apartment I lived in with Tina, Ray, and her sons wasn't really accessible. It was on the second floor. I felt bad and guilty because they carried my wheelchair and me up two flights. I didn't get out much because of this situation. It didn't bother me too much since I knew how to occupy my time. I started writing a little bit.

Tina's friends were just like her and made me feel welcomed. They love to have fun and drink. They were very interesting people. I loved that they had their own unique style and philosophy of life. I learned a lot from them.

Tina gathered information so I could become independent. The agency she found was similar to the state vocational rehab in New York and North Carolina. At first I was skeptical, but then I realized that I had good success with them in North Carolina. I gave it a chance.

The agency was far beyond my expectations. I had a great counselor. She got me an electric wheelchair. I was able to be more independent and was able to explore on my own. I loved it. The agency installed an electric door opener so I could enter and exit on my own. The agency also introduced me to the Consumer Directive Personal Assistance Program.

I was very curious about this program. Basically I was able to hire and fire whoever I wanted, and they got paid through a home-health agency. Medicaid paid the agency, my employees. This gave me more freedom to live my life the way I wanted it to be. I was so happy.

I was extremely ecstatic when Tina was able to get me into my own handicapped apartment. I was very worried about how I was going to pay for this because of my limited financial situation.

I had reservations running through my mind. I was worried that I was not going to be able to succeed in this endeavor. The most important thing that was worrying me was who was going to work for me besides Tina. I didn't really know enough people to help me every day. She eased my worries by informing me that her friend Stacey would work for me during the day, and she could work for me at nighttime.

When I first moved in, I was nervous because one way or another, I either lived with family or had an irresponsible roommate, but I realized that this would be different. It was different but in a good way. It didn't take long for me to think positively. Everything in my apartment was mine. I didn't have to answer to anyone. I didn't have to compromise with anyone. It felt great.

Stacey and I got along very well. She was a great friend as well as a home-health aide. She was very intelligent and talented. We had some things in common. For example, we both liked to write and listen to a variety of music. She had other interests that intrigued me.

Stacey was heavily into witchcraft and tarot cards. When I found this out, I'm not going to lie, part of me was scared. On the other hand, I found myself very impressed and curious about the subject. I thought, *Could this really be possible?* The only witches I had seen were on TV.

I loved when she did the tarot cards on me. At first, I was very skeptical and a nonbeliever. I thought the only person who knew what was going to happen to me was God. But at the same time, God also gives people the gift to show a glimpse of someone's life. She made a believer out of me right away. Whatever she told me always came true. Maybe not the next day, but within three months, it came to light.

I used to love hanging with her outside of work too. I remember the first time I met her family, I was nervous. I never know how people and children will react to my disability. Fortunately for me, everybody was polite. The kids didn't ask me any questions about my disability. Even in my late twenties, sometimes it was difficult for me to explain.

One of the best times in my life was hanging out with Stacey and her family. At first, I thought I would be nervous being at her apartment without Tina and Ray, but I was surprised how comfortable I was. The good thing was usually they showed up. It was fun drinking, talking, and watching everybody play cards, especially after her children went to bed. I used to sleep over at her house from time to time. Some of my best tipsy moments were at her house.

When I first came to Maine, I thought that Tina was only going to make sure that I was comfortable, and then she was going to disappear and live her own life. In my defense, from 1998 to 2001, people had let me down. I was fortunate that I had a bunch of reliable people to call upon.

While in Maine, I kept in constant contact with Veronica and Patty. I didn't want them to worry. I made sure that everything was going to be all right. I felt more at home in Maine than I ever did in New York and North Carolina. Deep down, I didn't think that Tina was going to let anything or anyone hurt me. I felt truly loved.

Tina and her family included me in everything. For instance, they invited me to birthdays and holidays. I loved being with them during those times because it reminded me of when I was younger. I'm not going to lie; I missed those days.

I was also very touched when they included me on family trips. For instance, when they took me to Story Land. I had a great time since there were a lot of us: Tina and her family, Lynn and her daughters, Missy and her husband, Gunner, with their daughters and Rose and Dickie. It reminded me of when my family and their friends went to Six Flags.

Tina and her sisters convinced me to go on the water rides. I'm always worried about putting my trust in other people, besides my family, when it comes to water rides. I always think; *will they be strong enough to hold me?* I didn't want to get injured. But in the long run, I had nothing to worry about. She and her sisters lifted me into the canoe. I went on it twice. Tina and her sisters were in the canoe. The first time, Tina held me, and then Lynn did it. I forgot how much fun water rides in amusement parks were. I even have a picture of us going down it.

Another fond memory that I have was going on a dirt bike with Gunner. I had never been on one. It was exhilarating. Part of me was worried, and part of me was eager with anticipation. I was curious how we were going to do this. They figured out a plan. They strapped me in front of him, and he held me tightly while he drove. At first, he started slowly, but as I got comfortable, I encouraged him to go a little faster. It was one of the best rides I ever took.

Another great memory that I recall was when Tina and Ray took me tube sledding. I had never heard of such a thing. They explained it to me, and I was like, "That doesn't sound like much fun." They convinced me to try it. I have to admit, curiosity got the better of me.

Tina and Ray put me in a tube. Ray dragged me up a mountain. Once I got up there and looked down, that was a whole different situation. I was scared out of my mind. There was no way I was going to do it. They tried to reassure me that I wasn't going to fall out of it. It was funny. While Ray was distracting me, she pushed me down it. Ray was able to catch up to me in his tube and was able to guide and stop me at the same time.

They were curious about my reaction. I couldn't find the words to describe what I was feeling. Part of me was petrified, and another part of me felt alive. They knew I would like it. I wanted to do it again.

After a while, Tina and I were figuring out my future. I wasn't too thrilled to pursue an education, so I opted to find employment. Through one of her connections, she heard that a company was hiring. It was a telemarketing company. She encouraged me to do it. I thought I wouldn't be able to do the job efficiently.

I was astonished and appreciative that a company took a chance on me, especially when I had no work experience. I couldn't believe I found a job at thirty years old.

I went into this new experience with trepidation. I didn't really know what to expect. Like anything else in my life, people had to get used to my disability. Once they did, my coworkers and my supervisors were very accommodating.

At first, I had a little difficulty getting used to the routine. They first put me on outbound calling. I didn't understand what that was to be. I had to call customers to switch to AT&T. I hated it. I got frustrated when potential customers hung up on me.

I remembered thinking that they were going to fire me for not doing my job adequately. They must have seen that I was struggling but was determined. They decided to switch me over to inbound. Inbound calling was a lot easier for me. All I had to do was calm the customers down and fix their problems. I figured that I could do it.

There was an opening for a four-to-midnight shift. There was a pay differential. I jumped at the opportunity. I loved the night shift crew. There were only four people. It was hectic from four to nine, but after nine, it slowed down. We were able to do anything as long as we answered calls.

I couldn't believe how comfortable I was at doing my job. I did it so well that I got a certificate for solving the most customers' problems for a month. I was shocked because I didn't think there was a contest. Everybody was so proud of me. Truth be told, I was proud of myself.

At the time, I thought life couldn't get better than this. Even though everything was going well, I felt that there was still something missing. I wanted my girlfriend to come visit me. I wanted her to see I had made a life for myself.

Veronica came to visit me in Maine. It felt right. I introduced her to some of my friends. She loved it because we had privacy and she could be independent. It was also great that we didn't have to spend money on a hotel. It felt incredible to be able to go to work, come home to somebody, and then tell them about my day.

Veronica was torn about leaving me in Maine and returning to New York. I tried to persuade her to come live with me and we could build a future together. She wanted to, but she didn't think she could leave her family. It broke my heart every time she left. I wanted her to stay, but at the same time, I understood her predicament.

It took me a few days to get out of my funk whenever she left. My apartment was lonely without her. It was great going to bed together and then waking up beside her. I hid my disappointment from everybody.

I distracted myself with work, my writing, and my friends. I started to hang out with one of my coworkers outside of work. She was such a great lady. She made going to work enjoyable. We formed a unique bond. But with so many distractions, I felt like I was lonelier than usual. I wanted to be around people all the time.

My worker introduced me to her family. Her husband, at the time, was one of the coolest men in the world. I loved that he was a stay-at-home father. He definitely was no pushover, but at the same time, he was very helpful. We had a lot in common.

At the time, this was what I thought I needed. I wanted to live with a family again. I decided to move in with them. Tina felt that I was making a huge mistake, especially only knowing them for a few months. After I moved out of my apartment, she didn't talk to me for a little over a year.

I was heartbroken that I didn't keep in touch with her. I thought just because she didn't approve of my decision, she would at least make sure that I was all right.

I had to get used to a life without her. At first, living with my coworker and her family was great. The three of us got into a routine. My coworker's husband would help me with my hygiene. She and I would go to work, depending on our shifts. We settled on a reasonable agreement for rent. We'd come home, eat dinner, and the adults would hang out. I was thinking this was a satisfying situation.

Veronica came to visit me. Everybody welcomed her with open arms. My coworker's husband would keep her occupied while I was at work. I was so fortunate to have him around. I always felt guilty when she came because I would be at work. They wanted to help us build a future together. They wanted to build a little cottage on their property for us.

While I was living with them, tragedy hit my family. My aunt Geri died of cancer. I was devastated and frustrated. I couldn't believe yet another person that I was close with had passed away. I felt guilty that I couldn't attend the funeral. She wasn't just a family member; she was someone I considered a friend.

When I first heard of her passing, I was numb. I didn't know how to react. I understood people react differently when someone they love passes. I started to get angry with myself for showing no emotions. Then three days after her passing, I was watching TV in my room when something caught me just right; I started crying. I cried for thirty minutes alone in my room. I didn't tell anyone.

I made one of the most difficult choices in my life; I decided to leave my friend's home and thought it was time to be on my own again. It was time to let them be a family again. Besides, the house was getting crowded and hectic. They weren't too pleased that I left unexpectedly. I tried to give them a reasonable explanation. With the assistance of Tina and Ray, I vacated the premises.

I lived with them again. I had to be honest; I missed her and her family. Even though my coworker and her family treated me really well, I just never felt connected like I did with Tina's family.

I thought I needed to be constantly around family. But honestly, I needed to be by myself. I knew deep down everything would work out because I knew my aunt Geri was watching over me.

Tina found me yet another handicapped accessible apartment to live in. This time, I wasn't so apprehensive about living on my own. She found another friend to be my home-health aide. Tina also was my aide again. It was great since we had such a great rapport.

I felt everything was going smoothly. I had a new job. I loved my apartment. This time, I was more adventurous than where I previously lived. I met various tenants and even got close to some of them.

I formed a unique and tight bond with a man named Bruce. He was a lot older than me. I don't understand what it is with me with people older than me. I think it's because I was exposed to different generations while I was growing up.

Bruce and I went everywhere in our electric wheelchairs. He introduced me to everyone in our small town. It was great.

I used to love venturing out in my electric wheelchair. I used to go visit Tina at her second job. Sometimes I would inform her that I was coming, and other times, I'd just show up. She would tell me to call her when I was coming and when I got home. There were times that I forgot to do it.

Living in a small town had its advantages. For example, I would stop and make small talk. I used to love ordering from my favorite little restaurant. They would give me a little extra when I wanted to substitute something off the menu.

I was thinking the time was right to persuade my girlfriend to move to Maine. I tried to explain to her that leaving her family was going to be difficult, but she had the fortitude to achieve it, especially if she believed it. I also wanted her to believe in me as well as our love and that I wouldn't let anything happen to her.

To my surprise, she finally said yes. I was overcome with joy that she was ready to build a future with me. I knew it was a monumental leap of faith to follow her heart. She loved and missed me a lot.

Once she got to Maine, she kept in constant contact with her family. Deep down, she knew she had made the right decision. She loved that she had her own independence. She loved playing bingo and other board games with Bruce and me and our friends. Even Tina and Ray took us out to the bar. Bruce and I put all of her doubts out of her head. Things were going pretty well for us when an unfortunate health issue occurred in Veronica's family.

Her uncle developed cancer, and his health was fading quickly. She desperately wanted to see him before he passed on. I decided to go with her for moral and emotional support. We went to New York.

It felt strange being back in New York, considering I had not been back in seven and a half years. While visiting, I stayed with my brother John.

I made the best out of a bad situation. While my girlfriend was dealing with her uncle's ordeal, I got reacquainted with some of my family. By now, the only family I had left in New York was John and Patty.

I couldn't believe how fast things changed. Joanne, now my ex-sister–in–law, was still the same. I'm glad her personality didn't change. She always did know how to make me laugh. She was still a great cook. I thought it was going to be weird or uncomfortable to meet her new husband, Jeff, but it wasn't. He was nice to me. I'm glad that Joanne and my niece and nephew were fortunate to have him in their lives.

I couldn't believe how much Melissa, my niece, and Joey, my nephew, had grown. The last time I saw them, they were children. I felt guilty about not keeping in touch with them. I'm glad they turned out to be good kids.

Even though, I had a different kind of bond with Melissa than Joey, I tried to treat them equally. My number-one priority at the time was getting to know them individually. With Melissa, I found it interesting that her personality was unique. Her personality had a little bit of her parents in her.

Melissa was just like all the other women in my family. I couldn't believe how fast we bonded. I tried to not lecture her when she got in trouble or if she asked for my advice. I tried to always be honest with her on any topic. For the most part, she always listened to me.

My nephew Joey and I got along very well. We would watch TV or we would wrestle with each other. I couldn't believe how strong he was at thirteen years old. What amazed me the most about him was he would always assist me without any hesitation. In some ways, he was mature for his age.

While I was reconnecting with my family, I kept in constant contact with my girlfriend. I always reminded her that even though we didn't see each other much, I was just a phone call away. I would always be there for her. She appreciated my love for her.

Veronica and I stayed in New York for a week. We both felt sad that we had to leave the people we love. It definitely was difficult for her to leave while her uncle was in the hospital.

We came back to Maine and resumed our life. Every day, she kept in touch with her family. I hated to see her so distraught over this. I wanted to take the pain away. Three days later, we got that dreaded phone call saying her uncle lost his fight to cancer.

When someone passes away, I never really know what to say or how to feel. For the most part, I'm glad that person isn't in pain anymore and he or she is in a better place. But you feel like a piece of you dies with them, especially if you are close to them.

We returned to New York, and I stayed with John again. She stayed with her family. I wished that I were able to accompany her to her uncle's funeral. Unfortunately, there was no feasible way to do it. I didn't want to ask her family because they had other important things on their mind. Sometimes life just isn't fair.

At the time, I didn't understand her religion. There were certain beliefs and rituals that she had to go through. I wasn't sure how long it would last. I thought we would only be there for a week … tops.

I wanted to be a supportive boyfriend. I tried to convince my girlfriend there was no way we could stay in New York no more than a week. I had a life back in Maine and responsibilities. She was very torn between her family and me. I wanted to know, if I left, would she return to our life in Maine? She honestly didn't know the answer to the question.

She knew she loved me, but she felt like her family needed her more. She felt like if she left, she would be abandoning them. In Maine, she wouldn't have felt close to her uncle. She said she probably would return to Maine, but she didn't know when.

Part of me respected her devotion to her family, and I was a little envious of her for having that kind of family dynamic. Deep down, I knew I couldn't tear her away from them. If I forced her to choose, she would've never forgiven me. I couldn't live with myself if I did that. My philosophy is I didn't come into her life to make it difficult. I always wanted happiness for her.

A part of me despised New York. I left New York for a reason. I hadn't lived in New York in seven and a half years. I went to visit a few times. I never thought I would live there again. It was very difficult for me. Even though I had some truly monumental events there, it hadn't felt like home in a very long time. I was thinking, *what does a man in my position do?*

I contemplated my dilemma for a long time. In 2004, I did the most unselfish thing in my life; I decided to move back to New York. This was definitely the toughest decision I've ever made in my life.

Now I had to get my affairs in order. I had to ask my brother John if I could come live with him. He asked if this was what I wanted to do. I told him this was what I had to do. He must have been satisfied with my answer because he said yes. I was thankful he came to my rescue.

Another thing I had to do was tell Tina my decision. Again, I felt horrible doing this to our friendship. I tried to convince her that for six and a half years, my girlfriend traveled back and forth; it was the least I could do. She thought I was sacrificing everything for someone who didn't deserve it.

I tried to persuade her that it wasn't because she didn't deserve it; it was because she led a different lifestyle than we did. It was really the circumstances that dictated her life.

I really didn't want this decision to affect our friendship. Besides Veronica, she was the most constant thing in my life. I will always be thankful for everything she did for me. Even though she didn't approve, she wished me luck.

From 2004 to 2010 were some of the darkest times in my life. So many things went wrong that I never expected to happen. There were a lot of false accusations, mistrusts, and misunderstandings. These years definitely tested my faith and my patience.

It was very difficult for me acclimating back to New York. Everywhere I went there was one obstacle after another. I thanked God that my brother John was there for me. Living with him was like old times. Our routine was still the same. We lived like bachelors. Most of the time, we ordered out.

I got to see Melissa, Joey, Jeff, and Joann more often. Most of the time, Joann made sure that my brother and I ate other things besides Chinese and pizza. She didn't want us to eat crap all the time. Partially, she was right, but we loved it anyway.

When my brother was at work, sometimes my niece and nephew would stop by after school. I was grateful because after a while, I would go stir crazy. There was only so much TV, reading, and talking on the phone I could do. They would hang out with me a few hours a day.

It was cool when Joann included John and me on certain family outings. We went to several street fairs and carnivals. Everybody bonded very well. People might think that I wouldn't like street fairs or carnivals because I can't get on the majority of the rides, but it's just the opposite. I just love the ambiance of it all.

I loved it when Veronica came over to visit me. I introduced her to Joann, Jeff, Melissa, and Joey. Everybody treated her kindly. She always loved being around my family because of the way they treated me.

It was even cooler when she went to Pennsylvania with John, his two kids, and me. I thought she would be nervous to meet the rest of my family, but she wasn't. Everybody stayed at Barbara's house.

It was great seeing everybody. It was definitely interesting to see my mother in Pennsylvania. I was happy that country living suited her. She made friends and started a daycare center with Barbara.

I was happy to see my other nieces and nephews. I couldn't believe how many years went by. The last time I saw them was when they were children. Part of me felt old.

I'm glad that I was able to bond with them. My relationship with Michael picked up right where we had left off. I couldn't believe how much he had grown; he was in his late teens and very responsible.

My niece Caitlyn turned out to be a very outspoken and sweet girl, and she looked just like her mother. We bonded very well. She had such confidence and conviction for someone so young.

I knew Barbara was going to raise her children right. I'm proud that she did it all by herself. She raised her kids the same way she raised me—with love, fairness, and honesty. Every time I went to Pennsylvania, I stayed with her.

It was great seeing Dennis with his family. I was very nervous meeting his daughter for the first time. I wasn't really sure how she would react to my disability. To my surprise, she accepted me right away. She reminded me of myself when I was her age. She was very perceptive and observed everything while reading her book. I knew Dennis would be a fun and loving father.

I met my sister Carol's husband, Joe, and their son, Joey. My brother-in-law is a funny man and treats my sister well. I'm glad that she found someone to spend the rest of her life with.

It was great to see my aunt Carol and her family. My cousin David is still the same. He's still one of the funniest men I know. His son, Brendan, is just as smart as his father. Just like his father, he's built like a rock but wouldn't hurt a soul. My cousin Mary looked like she enjoyed the country life.

At the time, I was glad that I got reacquainted with my family. Everything was going smoothly for me, and then I hit a roadblock. The house that John and I lived in was being sold, and we had to get out. John tried his best to search for a ground-floor apartment for both of us. Unfortunately, he didn't find one. I didn't know what to do.

I knew that I couldn't live in the mountains where my family members live. Their houses weren't accessible for me. Besides, no one offered anyway. The weather in Pennsylvania sometimes was worse than New York. It snowed six months out of the year. I would be stuck. I became discouraged.

I couldn't believe the one person who came to my rescue. Veronica asked her parents if I could come live with them. To my surprise, they agreed to it. I was so relieved.

I'm not going to lie. I was a little nervous moving in with them. I'd only met her family a few times, but we just made small talk. Living with them was going to be an interesting experience, but like everything else I did in my life, I did it with an open mind.

Veronica and her family will always have a special place in my heart. God bless their souls because they made me feel special and tried their very best.

I have to admit living with them wasn't always easy. The house wasn't very accessible. Lucky for me, I was used to climbing stairs and lifting myself onto furniture and into my wheelchair.

Everybody had to adapt to each other. They had to adjust to my disability, and I had to get used to the language barrier. For instance, Veronica's parents spoke very little English.

Her parents were very special and loving people, and they treated me very well. Her mother taught me words in their native language. She was an excellent cook. Veronica's father was a very kind man and never raised his voice. He would do the best he could for anyone. For instance, he did everything he could to find me an accessible place to live. After a while, the language barrier wasn't really an issue. I loved them like in-laws.

Veronica's brother and his ex-fiancée and I formed a unique bond. Her brother was a good guy. He was definitely passionate about his beliefs. Sometimes our beliefs in life would clash. He considered himself a conservative, and I consider myself a liberal. It was interesting because whenever a topic came up at the dinner table, it would usually be her brother's views against his ex-fiancée and me. My girlfriend would translate for her parents. Lucky for me, I love a good debate.

Her brother and I didn't always clash. There were good times too. I loved that he liked to dress well. He also taught me about the stock market and even bought *Stock Market for Dummies* for me. The book was interesting to read.

While living with my girlfriend's family, I saw her in a new light. I never understood why she couldn't leave New York and live with me in Maine. Her parents made a person feel safe and welcomed, so it could really be hard to go into the real world. It could be difficult for someone who has been sheltered her whole life.

While living with her, Veronica taught me what true courage meant. Her disability was very stressful, but you would never realize it by looking at her. I was always in awe of the way she handled everything. She always had a smile on her face and only showed fear to certain people. If it were anyone else, they would be mad at the world. To be honest, I don't think I could've done it.

While I was living at my girlfriend's house, her brother got us into the life insurance business. Never in my wildest dreams had I considered entering that profession. At the time, I was trying to better my financial future and be able to take care of my girlfriend the way she was accustomed to. Any risk that I took, I always had her in mind. I decided to look at this endeavor as a great opportunity.

The life insurance business wasn't what I thought it would be. There were mitigating circumstances that hindered my success. You have to be a very persuasive and intrusive person. I felt very strange asking people about their financial as well as their personal lives.

Even though I had my doubts, I tried my very best. Veronica and I tried to be relatable to the people who trained us. There was a lot of material to absorb. Some of it was easy to comprehend while other subjects were not.

The one positive aspect of doing this business was that you were able to recruit your friends. For instance, I was reunited with my camp buddy, Frankie. He and I had a major disagreement in the 1990s. I was very excited that he was interested.

Frankie and I had to start over, but it was worth it. Luckily, it didn't take long for us to overcome our issues. We had the same philosophy in life. The life insurance involved two great things that we loved: money and helping people.

Veronica, Frankie, and I were like the three musketeers. We trained, studied, and recruited together. One of the toughest parts of the life insurance business is the letdown. For instance, people would agree with the plan but then change their mind at the last minute. Unfortunately, we had more people turn us down than taking the plan. Her brother and his ex-fiancée tried very hard to enhance our confidence.

After we finished our training, Frankie and I had to take our New York State Life Insurance test. Now that was the toughest test I ever took. No matter how much material you think you know, it's still not enough. The first time I took it, I thought I passed it, but I was wrong. The second and the third time, I did worse than the first time.

I was really starting to doubt myself tremendously. I was thinking; *why couldn't I pass it.* I was thinking about all the accomplishments that I had overcome in the past. I was determined not to give up. I prayed to God and trusted him to give me the fortitude to pass. On the fourth try, I thought I failed, but in reality, I passed. I was never so happy in my life.

While I was living at my girlfriend's house, I felt like I had a lot of stress to deal with. The only way I knew how to relieve some of that stress was to go to church. Church was a place where I could gather my thoughts and feel at peace. I went three months straight.

I found it interesting because my family wasn't really religious. The only time I went to church was either for a wedding or when I did my Catholic ceremonies. For instance, when I did my communion. I surprised myself because I didn't need anyone convincing me to attend. This is what needed to be done. I felt comfortable one hour a week to be myself. I knew God had a plan for me, and I had to trust him.

He led me to a path of finding some more of my friends from camp. Frankie found out that my camp was celebrating its one hundredth anniversary. He wanted to go, but I was very skeptical. I thought that part of my life was closed, and I didn't necessarily wanted to reopen it.

On the other hand, I would be lying to myself if I didn't admit I was a little curious to see how everyone turned out. Frankie told me who was going to be there, and I figured why not. Besides, I wanted to show Veronica where I spent my summers.

There were so many emotions that were going through my mind when I arrived. I couldn't believe Camp Oakhurst was around for a hundred years. I couldn't believe how much it had changed. It was nice sharing my experience with my girlfriend. She loved hearing the stories we told. The campers definitely behaved better than Frankie and I did when we were there. It was very interesting how the ethnicity had changed. There were more minorities there than when we went.

I also loved seeing some old friends and some acquaintances. I introduced Veronica to everybody. It was nice to see people I hadn't seen in years. I thought about them but didn't do anything about it.

It was interesting to see the dynamics between some of us. For instance, I was very close to one of the girls. Let's call her Yasmine. When we were teenagers, I always thought she was beautiful, and I had the biggest crush on her. But I didn't act on it. Instead I settled on just being her friend.

I wanted to get to know her as an adult. I met her husband. Let's call him Roger. After the mini camp reunion, Frankie, Yasmine, Veronica, Roger, and I started to hang out. For instance, we would go bowling or out to eat.

The relationship between Veronica and me started to get rough. There were so many things pulling us in different directions. I knew I had to fix it. I thought it was time to move out and find a place for us to live. I knew I wanted to save it because it was special to me.

Yasmine found a handicap accessible apartment to live in. Frankie, my girlfriend, and I went to see it. It was on Long Island.

It was a two-bedroom apartment on the second floor. I liked it. The apartments in Maine were better. I thought it would be a new beginning for Veronica and me.

Unfortunately, that wasn't the case. She didn't want to move in with me; she felt comfortable staying with her family. It hurt me because I wanted a future for us. But at the same time, I understood her situation. I reminded her that I didn't come into her life to complicate it. I respected her decision.

When I look back at my life in the apartment on Long Island, I wish I had done things differently. There were some good and bad things that happened. I should have trusted my instincts as well as listened to people's advice. I was mad at myself because I kept making the same mistakes over and over.

I had reservations moving into the building. First, I thought, *here we go again, moving into yet another building*. I got tired of moving. From 1998 to 2006, I moved several times, and I hated it.

Whenever I moved somewhere new, I kept a low profile to be private. I wasn't rude to anyone, but I kept to myself. I said hello or nodded my head. I tried to be more observant and cautious.

I also had to get used to the home-health aide situation again. I had to get used to the variety of attitudes that would be coming into my apartment. I had some good ones and some horrible ones. There were some who were proactive, and then there were some who were downright disrespectful. For instance, I had one who talked about her lifestyle loudly on the phone. I politely told her to speak quietly because the walls were extremely thin, and I didn't want my neighbors to hear.

She also made friends with my neighbor across the hall from me. She would get me ready for the day and then proceed to go to the neighbor and spend the next two hours gossiping. Needless to say, she didn't last long with me. I didn't need anyone disrespecting me or getting me into trouble with the building management office.

Little by little, I started making friends with the other tenants as well as the staff in the building. Through the gossip line in the building, I knew who to be nice to and whom I could trust. At first, I didn't want to trust anyone because of my experiences in the past.

When I moved into the building, I lived on the second floor. Some of the tenants were nice and quiet, while some of the tenants would play their music till late at night. It reminded me of my dormitory life in Pennsylvania. I became close to Mike, my next-door neighbor.

Mike and I had a lot in common. We had a similar family upbringing. He was a freelance writer. He used to give me tips on how to make my stories and characters come alive. We confided in each other. He became my best friend while I lived there.

Then the building management insisted on me moving to the first floor because my girlfriend didn't move in with me. The management's policy was that only couples or families were able to occupy two bedrooms. I hated moving again, but at least it was in the same building.

I was also close to an aide and her family. It started great at the building, but then it got complicated. There were a lot of issues we disagreed on. I mean she started to not take the job seriously. She would come late and leave early or go visit other people in the building. I began to get angry about the situation. I tried to express my concerns politely.

She didn't like what I was saying and began to get offensive and insulting me about my character. She insisted on reprimanding me for not understanding the black race. She insulted the way I was brought up and how I never dated a strong black woman. She also proceeded to persuade and try to make me understand what it feels like to be a black man in today's society. She thought it was a shame I thought I was better than my own race.

I will never understand why people have to throw the race card in my face once they find out how I was raised. It seems like society needs to categorize you in a particular way, and that's how they define you. I've heard all the insulting comments from "oh, I don't consider you black" because I have a white family to "you don't know how to act black."

I also always find it interesting that some people almost want me to apologize for being adopted. I feel like I shouldn't be judged by the color of my skin or disability. I want society to judge me for the things that I do. I wish people would stop stereotyping me into a particular category. I am a man who happens to be black and disabled.

Needless to say, I accept people for what they do and not the color of their skin. I love people who make an honest living and work hard. Anytime somebody new enters my life, I'm very cautious and observant until I get to know the person because most people have burned me.

Whenever the agency would send over somebody new, I always asked if the person could understand me and vice versa. I hated when the agency would lie and send people who barely spoke English. It definitely made it difficult and challenging to communicate throughout the day.

I had a unique bond with some aides. I recall bonding with a particular aide. We became very close. While she worked for me, she used to teach me Spanish and translate her soap operas into English for me. I always admired how she was able to do it. I met several members of her family. I wish I kept in touch with her.

There was also another aide that taught me Spanish words. I met her family members as well. She even trusted me to teach one of her sons English. I had my doubts because I never was a tutor to anyone. She paid me. I felt honored. I even became a mentor to him. To this day, I feel bad that I didn't keep in touch with them.

My life in New York started to go smoothly, not great but steady. I thanked God for providing me with food, shelter, and some good friends. I also had my girlfriend in my life.

I also reconnected with my uncle Tommy and his two daughters, Eileen and Lisa. By now, he was living in Arizona. We would correspond back and forth at least once a week. As for his daughters, we picked up right where we left off, as if I had never left New York.

I also thought that it was great when someone from my past moved into my building. He went to my camp. I never associated with him, but we knew each other. We had mutual friends. I remember people warning me to stay away from this individual. I thought that I had to form my own opinion.

Let's call my camp friend Rusty and his wife Hillary. At first, I found him and his wife a great addition to my life. He let me in and shared his experiences and projects he was interested in. I was amazed by how he was able to balance his personal time as well as his professional life.

Rusty, Hillary, and I had a lot in common and shared everything together. We would argue like we were brothers. Sometimes I felt sorry for his wife because she would play peacemaker. There were times that we wouldn't speak to each other for several days, and I knew it upset her.

Things weren't always difficult between us. There were a variety of things that I liked about him. I liked his tenacity and determination in accomplishing his goals. He could be very persuasive at times.

I liked Hillary. She was always kind and helpful to me. Whenever an aide didn't show up, she was always there lending a helpful hand. She even introduced me to her family. She invited me to her family's house during the holidays.

Together, they showed me a variety of different things. For instance, he introduced me to public speaking. I attended one of his speaking events. I loved it when he included me at one of these events.

I remember that he made it so easy to get in front of a large audience and discuss disability issues as well as his disability. When the time came for me to talk, he would come up with me and make me feel comfortable.

I remember thinking that the three of us made a great team. His wife would assist us with anything we needed. He and I would bounce ideas off each other. He was great at speaking to a large audience. I was great with words.

It wasn't always work, work all the time. Rusty helped me get back into wheelchair sports. I thought it was cool because I hadn't participated in anything athletic in over twenty years. He was a great athlete. He played wheelchair basketball, softball, and wheelchair soccer. Even though I know the rules to basketball, it was a hardship for me to push, dribble, and put the ball into the basket. Even though I didn't play, I loved watching it.

Wheelchair soccer was a sport that I wasn't familiar with. My camp friend thought it was a sport I would love and excel in. The more he described the sport, the more I was intrigued but hesitant.

He said that I could use my electric wheelchair to play. He taught me some of the rules. There are at least two motorized wheelchairs on a team. The electric wheelchairs blocked for the people who were in manual wheelchairs. The manual wheelchairs try to get the ball past the goalie and score.

Truth be told, I didn't think I would be interested. I went and tried it. I liked it. I hadn't been excited about participating in a sport since the New York marathon. I knew I had to get the concept of the game.

There were so many things that I had to be aware of. I had to learn the drills. I had to be aware of my teammates as well as the opponents from the other team. I realized that other motorized wheelchairs were powerful and quicker than mine. The first year, I have to admit, I was average. Then once I found my rhythm, I was good and tried my best.

The great thing about this sport was I had a lot of people assisting and training me. My teammates and coaching staff were understanding and patient with me. I got along better with some of the members of my team than others.

What I also loved about playing wheelchair soccer was it was very competitive. Everybody took it seriously. It was a league, and we got to travel and meet other disabled people. We even got trophies. Fortunately for me, I was on the winning team three out of the four years that I played.

From time to time, I think about my friendship with my friend and his wife. I think there were a lot of factors that contributed to the downfall of our friendship. For instance, we spent too much time together, and we became too intrusive in each other's lives. I believe we were too stubborn for our own good. We should've been happy for each other's accomplishments instead of envious or selfish.

Throughout this ordeal, my relationship with Veronica started to suffer tremendously. She despised my friends, except Frank. She thought they were getting in the way of us. She began to stay away more.

Whenever we did spend quality time together, it just didn't feel the same like it used to. There were more arguments and silence. I tried to have patience and be supportive.

But unfortunately, we hit a crossroads in our relationship. I never dreamt in my wildest dreams it would have come to this conclusion. Toward the end, there were too many distractions and a lack of communication to salvage our relationship.

Breaking up with my girlfriend was one of the toughest decisions I ever had to make. I didn't make this decision lightly. I had to take into consideration the ten years we spent together.

For the most part, we were happy when she visited me in other states. Part of me realized that being back in New York was going to be difficult. I never realized the emotional aspect as well as the obstacles that could stand in the way of the happiness.

There was a song Ralph Tresvant sung called "Do What I Gotta Do" that reminded me of the situation with Veronica. The chorus described the way I was feeling. The line was "Do what I got to do and break her heart. I don't want to see her cry, but it's hard to live a lie."

Even though I thought this is what I needed, I didn't want to hurt her. I loved her, but I was no longer in love with her. My heart and mind were not in the same place. I had to be truthful to myself as well as to us as a couple.

After my breakup with my girlfriend, the last thing I was looking for was to jump into another relationship. Sometimes things don't always work out the way you want them to. I met this lady through a mutual acquaintance of Yasmine's. Let's call her Kiera. I met her twice. The first time, she was dating another camp acquaintance that I knew. The second time was when a bunch of my friends hung out at Dave and Buster's. I thought she was so pretty, and I couldn't keep my eyes off of her.

When Kiera broke up with her boyfriend, she and I started to hang out with each other. I always looked forward to spending time with her. At the beginning, there was more laughter than sadness. I found it refreshing for someone to open up about their disability.

To be honest with you, at the time, I wasn't familiar with her disability. She told me about it, and it didn't matter to me. At the same time, I also did research on the topic. I wanted to have as much knowledge as possible. I found being with a person with her type of disability could be challenging at times.

The more time we spent together, the more we realized that we had a lot in common. For instance, we loved watching movies and loved watching the behind the scenes and reading the credits of movies. To this day, there aren't many people I've met who share that experience with me.

I have to admit never in my wildest dreams did I think that we would be more than just friends. On my part, the more time I spent with her, the more I liked her, but I wasn't sure if she felt the same way. Then one day, my dreams came true. She reciprocated the sentiment.

There were so many obstacles as well as people who were totally against our relationship. What people didn't comprehend at that time was that we balanced each other out. Everybody thought we didn't know what we were doing. They thought that we were opposites in every way possible. In some respect, they were right. But in other ways, they were wrong.

I learned a lot from Kiera. I learned that just because you are financially comfortable doesn't mean you're happy. She also showed me not to take life so seriously because I tend to be rigid. Around her, I could relax to some extent.

She learned from me that there are men who could handle her disability. There are men who would take the time to listen to her opinion. She is very intelligent, but not a lot of people give her the confidence for her to express herself. I assisted her in finding a support group for her disability. I also made sure she took her medications regularly.

The biggest obstacle was her parents; they didn't understand what she was doing with me. They thought that I was taking advantage of her. They also didn't like my disability and my color. This was a shame because anyone who knows me realizes that is not the case. They started to put doubts in her mind.

The problem with putting doubts in Kiera's mind was it took a big toll on her emotionally. She was torn between her parents and me. I tried to tell her things that I thought were good for her, and then they would want her to do things their way.

I felt horrible for her because it put her in a tough position. She had to find a happy medium between her happiness with me and being loyal to her family. While I was dating her, it reminded me of my relationship with Veronica. Another relationship where I felt like my girlfriend couldn't stand up for what she wanted in her life.

While dating Kiera, I realized that I needed to prioritize my life again. Rusty introduced me to Suffolk Independent Living Organization (SILO). I didn't really know what this organization did.

SILO is a nonprofit organization that helps people with disabilities have the same rights and responsibilities, desires, and needs as their nondisabled peers. I thought, *Wow, this is what I need in my life.* I needed an organization to show me the direction I needed to go.

I went with Rusty and Hillary to a meeting. I was very impressed, and I learned a lot from them. We became close to a lot of their members. For instance, there was a woman who was very knowledgeable and vey nice. She treated us with respect and didn't talk down to us. I needed someone to mentor, empower, and advocate for me if I needed assistance with my life.

I wanted to do positive things in the community. I didn't want to sit down and collect Social Security benefits for the rest of my life. I remembered that I was more proactive when I was in my youth. I wished I knew this nonprofit organization when I was growing up because I believed my life would have taken a better course than what it had become.

I recall thinking I had to stop feeling sorry for myself and move forward. I also thought that nothing gets accomplished if I keep on concentrating on my past. I could learn from my mistakes. I absorbed as much information from them as I could.

The first thing I did was to see if there was a CDPAP program in New York. I didn't want to rely on a home-health agency anymore. I was getting frustrated with the home-health agency sending people who couldn't speak English very well or disrespecting me.

I felt empowered. Now I could hire and fire whomever I wanted. The problem was whom would I be able to hire and trust. It wasn't like it was in Maine. I contemplated this issue and discussed it with my uncle Tommy.

I wished I knew then what I know now. But unfortunately, I had to learn things the hard way. I didn't know as many people to work for me like I did in Maine. Truth be told, I didn't have Tina picking out responsible people for me. My options were limited. I turned to my friends and Kiera to be my aide.

Initially, I had doubts about hiring my friends and my girlfriend over strangers. I didn't want my friends to know everything about me. But I thought, *how difficult could it be?* I was able to balance my personal life and professional life in Maine, so why couldn't I do it in New York?

It was more difficult than I ever imagined. In New York, I had to deal with more petty issues as a boss. I only hired three of my friends, but that was enough to last a lifetime. For instance, I had to deal with them complaining that one was doing more than the other. I tried to be impartial and objective when I listened. I also divided up the tasks as equally as I could.

Sometimes the friendship and the role of employer got blurred a little. My friends who worked for me didn't take the job seriously. It was also difficult for Kiera to distinguish between being my aide and when to be my girlfriend. I was torn and felt guilty for reprimanding them. I saw that my friendships were being affected by this situation.

I thought the best course of action was to keep only my girlfriend as an aide and hire a complete stranger to assist me. At the time, I didn't want to do it. But that was my only option. I interviewed plenty of people before settling on a person. I was hoping that we would be compatible and that I could trust them.

Over the years, I had to hire and fire many people. I found that people had great work ethics for about a month, and then their true personality appeared. For instance, I had one lady who brought her husband and granddaughter to work every day. I despised that because I felt that she wasn't taking the job seriously.

Another example was that I hired a lady as a favor for a friend. At first, the woman was fun to be around. We went to flee markets. Then she started to neglect her duties to me. When I fired her, she didn't take it very well. She started leaving obscene messages on my phone.

After those experiences, I tried to hire people through people that I knew so that they could vouch for them. I don't like when people take my kindness as a weakness. I have a lot of patience, but I don't like to be used.

Whenever I needed assistance with any issue, I always called SILO. They even recommended me to be a peer mentor to someone. I felt honored that they thought of me that way. I always liked helping people.

At first, I had my reservations about being someone's peer mentor. I thought you had to have professional training. SILO informed me all I had to do was to tell my experience as a person with a disability. I had the confidence to talk with a guy.

I met my new vocational counselor through my peer mentor program. She was very impressed with the way I handled her client. She thought that I should do this as a career. She wanted to be my new vocational counselor.

I told her my experiences with the vocational program. She was very empathetic and told me that the program had changed since the last time I was in it. At the time, she persuaded me to give her a chance. I felt she was very different from my previous counselors. She encouraged and listened to me.

I took a leap of faith again with the vocational program. I was hoping this time would be different. I felt confident with my new counselor. I thought she wanted the best for me.

Every time I participated in the program, I had to take a series of tests. These tests take three days to do, and they are tedious. They test you on everything from intelligence to your strengths and weaknesses.

It amazed me how surprised my counselors were when they got the results. I tried to make a joke out of it and usually said, "I'm smart when I need to be. I just don't apply myself as much as I should." They usually didn't know how to respond to my declaration.

What mystified me was when they would ask what I wanted to do for a living. I told them I wanted to do something in the entertainment field, specifically writing. They usually felt that was not a realistic goal. I didn't understand why they would ask, especially when they were going to try to dissuade me anyway. But I promised myself I wasn't going to be obstinate.

My counselor and I decided on a reasonable and acceptable plan. I knew I didn't want to go back to school. I decided I wanted to go back to work. I tried to tell my counselor that a lot of employers were not going to take a chance on me because they were going to judge me on my disability, despite the tax benefits they could receive from the government.

I searched long and hard for a job for a long time. I started feeling hopeless. When luck was on my side, I did go to job interviews but didn't get the position.

When I finally did get a job, I had my doubts. It was as an outbound representative for a telemarketing company. I was hesitant to take it because of my previous experiences.

I tried to inform my counselor that this job wouldn't be beneficial for me as well as for the company. She thought I was just being nervous and wanted me to think positive.

Against my better judgment, I took the job. At first, I went in there with a positive attitude. Deep down, I was petrified because I didn't want history to repeat itself. That didn't happen.

There were a lot of expectations put upon me. Not only did I have to fulfill the job tasks, I also had a job coach with me every day. The job coach was there to boost my morale whenever I needed it as well as to solve any problems with my employer.

At the time, I didn't need someone watching over me like I was some immature adolescent. I knew if there was a problem, I would be able to handle myself in a respectable and professional manner.

Every day, I would try to be optimistic. By midday, I started to get frustrated. I knew that if I didn't meet my quota, they would fire me. My job coach tried to help me, but nothing worked. I'm not one to give up so easily, but even I knew when to say enough is enough. I resigned after one week.

Needless to say, my counselor and job coach were not pleased with my conduct. They wanted to schedule an appointment with me. I realized this wasn't going to be a positive meeting. I tried to express my opinion and didn't want to attend. They insisted that they were there to help me and wanted to come up with a better plan for me.

Even though I was very leery as well as skeptical, I went to the meeting. I was willing to listen to their plan objectively. When I went to the meeting, all they brought up were negative viewpoints. I was very disappointed in the outcome and felt ambushed. When it was my turn to speak, I was polite but firm in expressing my point of view. I apologized profusely for not living up to their expectations. I reiterated that being an outbound representative was not my forte, and I had tried my very best. They thought I should have tried harder. I parted ways with the vocational agency again and thanked them for everything they tried to do for me.

After losing my job, my life seemed unfamiliar to me. Everywhere I turned, drama followed. I tried to avoid it, but somehow I got sucked back in. I realized some of it was my fault. Anytime someone had a problem, I would want to find a solution. Even though I would help people, they seemed to find a way to belittle or insult my intelligence. I started to doubt myself more than usual.

I knew I needed an outlet before I went completely insane. I joined Facebook to alleviate some of my frustrations. Facebook helped me to reconnect with family and friends. I was glad I made that decision.

Just like anything else in life, you form strong bonds with some old acquaintances, while others you just say hi whenever you can. I was thankful that I was able to reconnect with my second family from Maine. I'm also thankful that I was able to find Willie and Jason again.

I'm also thankful that Yasmine has always been there for me. I don't think I would have been able to get through the chaos without her. She also was going through some personal issues. We leaned on each other for emotional support.

When Yasmine resolved some of her personal issues, it was one of the hardest decisions she had to make in her life. She knew there were going to be ramifications from everyone. Even though it was difficult, she had to do what was best for her. She didn't make the decision lightly. She understood that a lot of people didn't agree with it. I stood by her and didn't sway her one way or another.

I had to take into consideration that Kiera and I were in a relationship. She and I were having problems of our own, and it was taking a heavy emotional toll on me. I wanted to try to rectify the situation.

For me, I needed to get away to clear my head and get a new perspective on my life. I discussed with the social director of my building what I was going through. She led me to believe that she understood my situation. I expressed my concerns about losing my apartment. She advised me to go clear my head and said I wouldn't lose my apartment.

Yasmine started her divorce proceedings, and she definitely wanted to move to Florida. She suggested that I go to Florida. I had my reservations about it, but I went anyway.

I left New York yet again. At the time, I had a good feeling about my decision. When I lived in Florida in the late 1990s, I loved it. I went to the state with an open mind and made sure I weighed my options.

Unfortunately, Florida wasn't as easy the second time around. There were positives and negatives of living in the sunshine state. For instance, the weather and people were pleasant.

Another positive was I was able to reconnect with my brother Timothy and my sister-in-law Shannon. We picked up right where we left off. I also got to meet my nephews, Patrick and Timmy. They are exceptional young men. They accepted me right away.

Another plus to being in Florida was that I was able to meet Yasmine's family. In some ways, her family was like mine. They treated her like she didn't have a disability. They reminisced with me about her as a child. Like me, she had responsibilities and got reprimanded when needed. I loved hearing these stories because it made me feel closer to her.

Unfortunately, there were some negative aspects of Florida. I tried to get personal care attendant services. I found out if I needed two or more daily tasks done, the state considered me nursing home eligible. It would have been easier for me to pay out of pocket. It would have been a financial hardship for me.

I also found transportation services difficult for me. I would have to ride longer on the bus than I did in New York. This would have been problematic for me because I wouldn't be able to go to the bathroom. It would have reminded me of when I attended John Jay College.

After a month and a half, the social director of the building in New York contacted me and told me my time was up. She said the building's lawyer would be contacting me by mail to give me the date in which I had to have my belongings out of the building.

I found this very alarming because I thought I had plenty of time. I didn't understand why there was an attorney threatening to evict me. I always paid my rent on time, even while I was in Florida. I tried to get a reasonable explanation from the social director, but all she kept on stating was that she could not discuss the case with me.

I was so perplexed about this situation because if I knew I had a time limit, I would have gone back sooner. In my opinion, they took drastic measures to remove me from the building without probable cause. I was an exceptional tenant and didn't cause any trouble.

I already was trying to figure out things in my head. This was an additional pressure for me. I didn't really want to leave my family and Yasmine in Florida. Even though I hit some roadblocks, I still was relaxed. At the time, I had to figure out where to put my things. I also had to call someone to pick me up at the airport.

Kiera picked me up at the airport in New York. She felt horrible about my troubles. She invited me to stay with her and her family. I knew that her family didn't like me very much so anything I told them, they figured I had ulterior motives For example, when they heard why I couldn't get back into my old building, they were skeptical. Her father was determined to get me back into the building but to no avail.

Kiera brought me to my old apartment. I tried to plead my case again to the social director. I tried to explain that I didn't have anywhere to go. She wasn't sympathetic to my plight. I couldn't understand the way she treated me.

After three weeks of living with her, her parents wanted me out of the house. I tried offering them rent. They didn't really give me any explanation on why I had to leave. They just wanted me gone. She felt torn, and it was making her depressed.

I realized that I couldn't return to Florida because it didn't have the services that I needed. My family wasn't an option; their houses were not accessible. Kiera assisted me in finding a place.

She and I even investigated shelters. We found out that someone with my disability wouldn't be able to survive in that environment. I couldn't have anyone come to help me with my personal needs.

I was starting to feel depressed since every avenue I pursued was not feasible. I even turned to SILO for assistance. They explored my options with me and suggested I temporarily find a viable hotel that could accommodate me, and then I needed to go to the Department of Social Services so they could assist me with the monthly bill of the hotel.

Kiera and I looked at a few hotels around her neighborhood. A lot of hotels said they were handicapped accessible, but they weren't. Either they were too small for my wheelchair to get around or the bathroom didn't have a walk-in shower for me. I began to get discouraged. Kiera's father kept on insisting that we needed to search harder.

Eventually he found an accessible hotel for me to live in. He paid for my first month's rent. I had to pay him back with my money that he was deducting from my Social Security income. I tried to negotiate with him to see if I could do smaller payment plans over several months but to no avail.

I went to the Department of Social Services for assistance. I have to admit, Kiera and I were very intimidated to go there. It was a long and tedious process. We were there all day. I was never assigned a particular counselor. Social Services ended up taking two-thirds of my Social Security check and gave me fifty dollars for food stamps. I was speechless.

How was I supposed to live on practically nothing? I had to make fifty dollars stretch for the month. I also had to still pay Kiera's father back. She tried to help me whenever her father allowed, which was rarely. She stayed at the hotel with me.

For the next three and a half months, there was a lot of pressure put upon me. I started to get depressed. My money was dwindling down to nothing. I ate a lot of frozen meals and had to use my money to do laundry.

Kiera's parents kept on insisting that she go home for a couple of days and leave me at the hotel. She was torn because she understood that I couldn't be left alone for a few days. She would go visit her family for a couple of hours and then return to the hotel.

I felt horrible for her dilemma. I tried to motivate her to the best of my ability, especially on the days we had to go to the Department of Social Services. I wished her parents and I could have come to some kind of mutual understanding. If we had worked together, it wouldn't have been tough on her. In the long run, she was pulled in opposite directions.

While I was staying at the hotel, I kept in constant contact with Yasmine and my uncle Tommy. They were my salvation. They felt helpless, but it was difficult for them to do anything from out of state. I always thanked them.

While staying at the hotel, there were so many negative thoughts running through my head. I was wondering how my life had gotten so disarrayed and complicated. I couldn't believe I was one step above being in a shelter or the street. I started hating everything about my life. I felt guilty for what I was putting Kiera through. She didn't deserve this.

I knew I had to do something before I lost my sanity. I didn't want to live in a negative state of mind anymore. The first thing I had to do was join the Nursing Home Transition Waver Program. SILO thought it was a good idea because it allowed me to stay out of a nursing home. They thought I was too young to enter one, and I had too much spirit.

I also started doing research on better and accessible living accommodations. I perused newspapers, used computers at the library, and looked at penny savers. I must have called about a dozen places and real estate agencies. I explained to them that I was on Section 8 and I paid a third of the rent and the state pays the rest. They were very skeptical about how they were going to get their rent.

I looked at several locations with Kiera and a SILO counselor. The places were either too small or too expensive. My SILO counselor tried to explain to landlords that if there were any modifications to be done, the state would do it for free. The landlords didn't want to do any renovations to their properties.

Every time I ended up back at the hotel, I felt hopeless. I even began to pray to God for help. I prayed that a landlord would take a chance on me. Then one day, He answered my prayers. A real estate woman came over to my hotel and met me. She was so heartbroken after hearing how I ended up there. I'll never forget what she said to me, "God has put us together for a reason." She also loved my spirit. To be honest with you, I thought I would never see this lady ever again.

Then three days later, she found landlords who were willing to meet me. At this time, I didn't want to get my hopes up too much because of my experiences dealing with landlords. My SILO counselor, Kiera, her mother, and I went over to meet them. I'll never forget meeting Gary and Aurelia Albert in January 2010.

Obviously, they weren't familiar with the waiver program, and they had to read about it. My counselor gave them all the necessary information that they needed so they could truly understand the situation. I thought after they read the material, they would change their minds, but they didn't.

I started bonding with my landlords. They invited me to all the barbecues, holidays, and any ceremonies they had at their house. I was so thankful that they said yes and were willing to take a chance. I think of them in the highest regards.

It felt good that I had a two-bedroom cottage that I could call my home. Even though it wasn't handicapped friendly, it was better than living in a hotel. I also knew that modifications were going to get done.

Another matter I had to deal with was that I had to change my attitude about my life and how to deal with people better. I decided if I wanted to have positive things happen to me, then I had to make the necessary moves to do it.

I decided that I needed to speak to a psychologist. At first, I wasn't sure if that was the best route to go. Society always put a negative stigma on people who went. I thought it was for crazy people. I knew I wasn't crazy but just depressed.

I took the leap of faith and went in with an open mind. It was the best decision I ever made. My psychologist is an exceptional therapist and has turned my life around tremendously.

She helped me see that I had a lot of unresolved issues. For instance, I had abandonment issues. It stemmed back all the way to when my biological parents gave me up. This is why I stay in unhealthy relationships.

Another major issue that I have is I put high expectations on people. I had to realize people have their own personal issues. If people do not take my advice, then I shouldn't take it personally. I don't need to be "Mr. Fix It" all the time. I found it ironic since my uncle Tommy had been saying it for years.

In my opinion, she was absolutely right. Since I am a caring person, I never like to see people hurt or cry, especially women. Most of the time, I brought drama into my life. If someone needs my advice or a shoulder to cry on, then that's great, but I don't need to solve their problems. Whenever someone wants to throw an olive branch at me, I'll take it.

Another major issue I had to overcome was the way I articulated my words. I always tried to be as honest as I could. I recall my mother saying to me that sometimes my honesty could be my downfall.

I never really realized that the way I formulated my opinions could affect someone's feelings. For example, I remember a friend of mine had a crush on me. She was curious to know what type of women I liked. I explained it to her honestly but not tactfully. Needless to say, I lost a great friend. I will always regret hurting her feelings. If I ever get the opportunity to see her again, I will apologize to her.

Another issue I had to figure out was I needed another aide to assist Kiera. She had a nervous breakdown and couldn't take the pressure that my life contained. I felt guilty since she was torn between her family and me. I couldn't do that to her anymore.

I found another aide who was more compatible. I met Amy through a mutual acquaintance. She has been a Godsend for almost four years. We have a great rapport with each other. She sees past the disability. She is smart, funny, honest, and a great listener. She is also very dedicated and has been there for me. I trust her implicitly, and I know she would never take advantage of me.

When she is going to be late, she notifies me and stays until her full shift is over. In my experience, this is very rare. Most aides would leave as soon as everything is done since they realize I'm capable of doing things on my own. Amy also defends me when someone is ignoring me. She had to put a lot of people in their places. She's like a second psychologist for me.

Nowadays, my life is a lot calmer then it used to be. I limit the drama to a minimum. Kiera and I parted ways amicably. She had to figure out how to make herself happy. I no longer could be an enabler to her unhappiness. We still keep in touch. I learned a lot about myself from her. I'll always be thankful for everything she did for me.

I've heard great relationships could come from friendships. I never really believed it could happen, especially to me. I thought it was just in romance novels and television. Or I thought it was a cheesy cliché.

For once, my life was going smoothly, but there was one key element missing in it. I had someplace to live, but it wasn't a home. Yasmine and I turned our friendship into a genuine relationship. It was the best decision we ever made. She moved in with me and made it complete. I understood with her by my side we could endure any obstacles as long as we had each other.

Another friendship I still treasure till this day is my cousin Eileen. As adults, we still make time for each other. We are fortunate to have partners who accept and love us unconditionally. I'm thankful that her husband, Chris, and Yasmine get along with each other. I'm happy that she has a little boy. She trusts me to hold him.

I also resumed writing my scripts. I no longer have anyone dictating how I should live my life. I understand that writing may not lead into a career, but I have to take a chance.

I read everything I can on how to write scripts. I absorb the material. I even entered myself in a screenwriting competition. In 2012, I was a finalist in the New York Screenplay Competition. Everyone was so proud of me. To be honest, I was also proud of myself.

It took me almost forty-two years to appreciate the things I have in my life. I appreciate my family for showing me what life is about and teaching me how to be independent. I'm no longer going to let anyone make me feel ashamed of the relationships that I have and will form in the near future.

If people believe I'm an inspiration, I respect their comments. It took me a long time to feel good about myself. I had to remember that life is too short. I also had to learn that if your mind and heart were not as one, then you would never truly be happy. I learned that there is no harm in trying. For me, I had to remember my promise to Juan and be the best I could be.

I had to learn that life has a lot of unexpected twists and turns. Unfortunately, I had to learn them the hard way. I also had to stop getting in my own way and creating unnecessary obstacles. The only thing I can do is face and overcome any challenges that come my way. I have the best support system anyone could ask for.

Printed in the United States
By Bookmasters